apples &
chalkdust

by
Vicki Caruana

Honor Books
Tulsa, Oklahoma

9th Printing

apples & chalkust:
Inspirational Stories and Encouragement for Teachers
1-56292-591-1
Copyright © 1998 by Vicki Caruana

Published by Honor Books
P.O. Box 55388
Tulsa, Oklahoma 74155

Dedicated to my husband, Chip,
and sons, Christopher and Charles,
for their gift of time

I would like to thank and acknowledge both
Anthony C. Horning and Ailene Doherty
whose teaching experiences and
insights were added to mine—
offering teachers everywhere
a chance to take a good, long look
at why we do what we do
at this place called school.

Introduction

Teachers all over the world share the bond of a unique profession. We possess the awesome responsibility and the distinct privilege of standing before our students not only as educators, but also as caregivers, counselors, and protectors.

Remember "judgment day"—the experience of standing before that first class of students and thinking, *Am I ready for this?*

I remember that day and the sudden realization: *I am the teacher.* And then the looming question: *What do I do now?*

At times, I still feel overwhelmed.

Other times awed.

At all times busy!

Many times I feel alone in my quest to give my best to my students. Yet, deep inside I know that I am not alone. Nor are you alone.

We teachers share a special bond. It is this bond, our shared passion for touching our students' lives, that enables us to understand each other. And through this understanding, we are able to offer each other friendship, expertise, and strength.

For all the teachers who are out there on the front lines, be encouraged. You are where you belong. I encourage you to persevere—for the students who look to you that first day of every school year with wide eyes and insecure grins.

Remember that our teaching is not for us. Our teaching is for them.

These stories, however, are for you.

Enjoy!

Vicki Caruana

"A teacher affects eternity; he can
never tell where his influence stops."
— Henry Adams

Jay

Maggie pulled her four-year-old son's hand a
little harder as she hurried him up the sidewalk. A
black pickup truck had slowed alongside them.

"Who's that, Mommy?"

"Let's keep walking," Maggie said. Not
recognizing the truck, she picked up the pace.

Just then her son tripped on a stray branch and
pulled on Maggie to wait. As she stopped, the dark
glass of the passenger window rolled down and a
young man with sunglasses leaned over to get a
better look at the sidewalk couple.

"Mrs. Jensen, is that you?" Maggie looked up,
responding with caution to the distantly familiar
voice. She scooped up her son and took a cautious

step back from the street.

The driver stopped the truck, put it in park, and excitedly ran around to meet her. Taking off his sunglasses so Maggie could see him better, he said with a touch of disappointment, "You don't remember me, do you?"

Apprehension turned to delight as Maggie finally recognized her former student. "Of course I do, Jay. You're a hard one to forget."

"I never forgot you, Mrs. Jensen. You're the only one who gave me a chance."

Looking at him she could still see the twelve year old who fought the system. As the big, black truck rolled away, Maggie smiled as she read his business card, "Jay Getz, Architect."

Even if the results of your labor aren't immediately apparent, take joy in the fact that your influence reaches further than you know.

Your successes may not show up in the classroom. Sometimes they show up when you expect them the least and need them the most.

"Experience is not what happens
to a man. It is what a man does
with what happens to him."
— Aldous Huxley

Space Shuttle

Hundreds of squinting eyes focused upward on a cloudless Florida morning. Teachers gathered and waited along with their students for the show to begin. It's always great to bring the classroom outdoors. It adds a real-life quality to the lesson.

Finally, waving hands began to point toward the eastern sky. Applause and cheers built to a roaring crescendo. It was a proud day for teachers and students alike.

"Go, Christa, go!" they cheered.

The space shuttle, disappearing into the

atmosphere, suddenly exploded, and its expanding cloud of debris streamed to the waiting ground below. The applause turned to questioning gasps and disbelieving screams. Teachers hurried their students back into their classrooms like a mother hen gathering her chicks. The questions were many. The answers were nowhere to be found. Although crisis teams descended on every school, children continued to look to their trusted teachers for stability and comfort. Teachers became mothers, sisters, friends, and counselors.

Doing what they do best—they taught.

They reestablished routine, and they prayed.

Whether it's war, scandal, or tragedy, you cannot shut the world out of your classroom. Every once in a while, the world's classroom crashes into your own. Handled well, even tragedy can teach the most valuable lessons.

Teaching to the situation allows the situation to teach to you.

"Change your thoughts and
you change your world."
— Norman Vincent Peale

First Class

Sandra had spent all weekend arranging and rearranging her classroom.

She decorated it with posters professing profound sayings. She set the desks in such a way that her students would receive the greatest impact from her teaching.

Finally, she sat on her stool at the front of the room and surveyed the setting.

It was perfect.

It had to be.

It was her first classroom.

Captivated by her own thoughts, she imagined

the events of the day to come. The student roster printed into her lesson plan book would come to life as the twenty-five sixth graders entered the room. The students, her students, would eye her warily as she moved to the front. She knew her carefully written name on the board would stump them. That was all right. She hoped its perplexing spelling would break the ice.

This was a moment she would remember all her life—a moment she had waited for and dreamed of since she was a little girl.

Sandra refocused on the still empty desks. With a heart full of hope, she prayed that this year would be filled with many significant and memorable moments for both her and her students.

What are your hopes and prayers?

On days when you wonder why you ever became a teacher, close your eyes and recapture the moment that inspired you long ago.

"The ultimate measure of a man is not
where he stands in moments of comfort and
convenience, but where he stands at times
of challenge and controversy."
— Martin Luther King Jr.

Picket Line

Vicki was well prepared for her new teaching assignment. However, it's never easy to start midyear. Squeezing through the adolescent crowd, Vicki approached her room. She was abruptly stopped by a picket line!

"No new teacher!" the signs glared.

Twenty-five sixth grade gifted students paced in front of her classroom, unhappy that they had been assigned to a new teacher. Without hesitation, Vicki slipped between the protesters, pushed the call button to the office, and reported the disturbance. Gathering her materials from the desk, she began to write assignments on the board.

Just then her principal stepped in to let Vicki know that her students were on their way.

A deep breath accompanied by a quick prayer was all she had time for.

As the now subdued crowd reluctantly entered the room, Vicki welcomed them with a spirited "Good morning!"

Their defiant gazes only barely met hers.

"We've got a lot of work to do, so let's get started."

Passing out some neon colored paper she said, "I'd like to work with you on creative problem solving. First we need a problem. Any ideas?"

Reluctant hands went up, and so began the process of building a new class.

Sometimes the only defense for skepticism and doubt you will have is your own self-assurance and poise. But there's no better way to restore trust.

Try to turn every situation, positive or negative, into a learning experience.

15

"Our task . . . is not to fix the blame for the past, but to fix the course for the future."
— John F. Kennedy

Seize the Day

Teachers know that the influence of a negative home environment can sometimes overwhelm their own ability to influence students in the classroom.

You can spend endless hours and days devising just the right incentive program or learning strategy. You can look for every opportunity to offer praise. Still, you can do just so much good during the few hours you have with your students.

Then they go home and spend fifteen to eighteen hours out of each day there—some without nourishing meals, love, attention, or encouragement.

These are the children we teach.

Sound defeatist? Not necessarily.

Consider the influence a child's friends can have on him. Parents continually worry that their children will follow the wrong crowd. While they may spend a great deal of time with their friends, it is still less than they spend with you.

Your efforts have more impact than you could ever realize. So much of what people are, can be attributed to environment.

Teachers are a part of each student's environment.

Become the most positive, encouraging part of your students' surroundings. When you do, school can become a life-changing experience. Show students the higher ground—they might just decide to aspire to it.

Don't let your concern for tomorrow keep you from making an impact today.

"Do what you can, with what you have,
where you are."
— Theodore "Teddy" Roosevelt

Little Budgets

Jan sat on the floor of her make-and-take workshop trying to decide on the most crucial thing to complete. The calendar math chart was done. She had already started the flannel board. She had six more projects and only an hour left in the session.

"I'll just have to wait until next month," she commented to a fellow teacher upon leaving the workshop.

Jan knew that money was tight in her district. Her first year of teaching was full of the unexpected. Her $100 budget was a meager offering. She still didn't have enough textbooks. Students brought in their own supplies. Paper was a treasured commodity. Jan didn't know any different; this was her first year. All she knew was if she wanted something, she had to make it herself.

She learned how to shop smart when ordering from supply catalogs.

She learned to glean from the wisdom of more experienced teachers to implement ideas.

She learned to be resourceful with what she had.

Jan's students didn't give a second thought to all the handmade accompaniments in their classroom. They *did* notice a creative and innovative teacher who touched their lives.

Model for your students how to make the best of any given situation.

> It doesn't really matter how big your budget is; what matters is if you are a good steward of what you've been given.

"Failure is only the opportunity to begin
again more intelligently."
— Henry Ford

Failed Lesson

John planned his study on multicultural
appreciation down to the letter. He gave his
students free reign when it came to presenting
their projects and envisioned all kinds of creative
multimedia presentations. With so many
interesting projects to choose from—he couldn't
wait to see what they would come up with.

Finally the day arrived and John began to call
the students up to make their presentations. After
five less-than-earth-shattering presentations, he
discovered that less than half of the class had
completed the assignment. It was obvious that this
was not just a typical situation.

Notes from frustrated parents were thrust in
his face.

What had gone wrong?

John decided to stop everything and find out why this lesson had become such an obstacle for his students.

He read the notes from the parents again and began to realize that he had overwhelmed his class with abstract guidelines and expectations. The idea was great. But John had to humble himself and admit to both the students and parents that he should have been more definitive in his expectations.

His humble attitude eventually earned him the loyalty of his students.

Allow creativity to define your projects, but be sure to clarify the guidelines for completing them. As a result, your students can exceed your expectations by courageously and creatively stepping out in their assignments.

If a great many of your students fail at some task, leave your pride at the door and look to yourself for solutions.

"Never, never, never, never, give up."
— Winston Churchill

Out of Time

At 6:00 p.m., Sally finally looked up from her computer screen. School was dismissed more than three hours ago, and Sally was beginning to feel the effects of skipping lunch. As the department head, it was up to her to complete an exhaustive report that had been sprung upon her at the last minute.

At 9:30 p.m., she called home to touch base and see if her husband had any trouble putting their two children to bed.

At 10:30 p.m., Sally was satisfied that the report was finally complete. She tried to print. She waited. Nothing happened. There was no ink in the cartridge.

Now what? she wondered. The office supply stores were closed. "Think Sally, think," she muttered to herself. Removing the computer disk, she hurried home. All the way she prayed that she would find an answer.

The next day Sally just couldn't focus on the morning routine. As she rushed to grab the car keys, her husband stopped her at the door. "Don't forget to drop this off," he said handing her the disk.

At that moment she realized the simplicity of the answer to her dilemma.

As Sally entered the school office, she approached her supervisor. "Here is the report you needed," she said as she handed him the disk.

As you work diligently, the most simple solutions usually reveal themselves.

You may not always be given adequate time to meet the expectations required of you. Work heartily. Stay focused on the task instead of the inconvenience it presents.

"The quality of a person's life is
in direct proportion to their
commitment to excellence."
— Vince Lombardi

Coaches

Ever wonder why coaches are so effective and
so loved by their players? *Coach* means *tutor* or
trainer. A good coach has high expectations,
encourages, and does more to "show" than "tell."

As teachers, we should take the opportunity to
learn from the efforts and focus of our school's
coaches. Coaches instill a sense of pride, a
cooperative spirit, and the competitive edge
necessary to win. Good coaches gain respect from
players and parents alike.

Good teachers run their game the same way. If

you want to lead a winning team, it's time you too became a coach. Yes, coaches sometimes have the advantage of choosing their teams, while teachers don't. But teachers, by inspiring students to achieve their personal best, have already won the game. Come alongside your students. Expect the best from them. Teach them never to settle for less. Spend more time showing and not just telling.

Your classroom is like the playing field. There are rules of play, scores to keep; there are victories, and yes, sometimes losses.

It's your job to train your students to perfect their game.

Take time to look at the winning team and find out what they do to win.

25

"One mother teaches more
than a hundred teachers."
— Jewish proverb

Frank Lloyd Wright

Frank Lloyd Wright's success as an architect was a direct result of the influence from his first teacher—his mother.

Like many of his contemporaries in the 1870s, Wright was schooled at home along with his siblings. His mother was always searching for opportunities to advance and improve the education of her children.

In 1876, the Wrights, taking advantage of the special railway excursion rates, traveled from Boston to Philadelphia to attend the Centennial Exposition.

At the Exposition, Mrs. Wright came upon a

life-affirming discovery for her son, Frank. The new Froebelian "Kindergarten" idea was on display, and Mrs. Wright eagerly drank in the new concepts and applied them to her children's education.

Although Frank was past kindergarten age, the Froebel ideas were quite formative for him, and he attributed much of his architectural success to his mother's wisdom and vision for his life.

As a teacher, never discount the incredible influence a mother has on her child's education. Allow her vision to reinforce your efforts in the classroom.

Strong parental involvement is key to the success of a child's education!

Be grateful for parents who involve themselves in their child's education. They can make your job so much easier.

27

> "Do the thing you fear and
> the death of fear is certain."
> — Ralph Waldo Emerson

Take Charge

Jayne's internship assignment in a high school seemed at first to be more intimidating than exciting. As she entered the school and forced her way through the crowd of 2,500 teenagers roaming the main hallway like an ocean of piranha, she felt sure she'd be eaten alive by the end of the first week.

Entering the classroom, Mrs. Randall graciously welcomed her and led her to a small desk on the opposite side of the classroom. "The kids will be here in about ten minutes. I believe in jumping right in, so as soon as the bell rings, you're on!"

Jayne's stomach was gurgling in protest.

Quickly arranging her materials, she stood at the front of the room and scanned the board for a piece of chalk.

The bell rang. She heard the shuffling of feet.

Jayne had no clue how to break the ice.

As frantic thoughts of what she should do or say next spun through her head, Jayne turned around just in time to see a paper airplane soaring by. She deftly caught the airplane in flight and without even thinking said, "Incoming!"

The students' critical stares immediately turned to grins of acceptance. With one confident move, she had captured the attention of her students.

And at that, Jayne relaxed and began to teach.

Remember that when you are put in charge—you must take charge.

"Encouragement is oxygen to the soul."
— George M. Adams

Balance

"Never smile before Christmas!" Most teachers know that there are some things you just don't do! And boundaries are a must when it comes to maintaining respect and order.

Common sense told Susan that it was easier to ease up on her discipline than to make it more strict. Yet, try as she might, she was unable to stick to that unwritten rule.

She loved children and wanted her kindergartners to have a sense of security.

She wanted her students to feel safe and to know that they could make mistakes without fear of humiliation.

She remembered well the embarrassment of having to stand with her nose to the chalkboard for an hour because she didn't know the answer to a math problem in junior high.

She did not want to produce that feeling in her students.

Susan believed, as so many teachers do, that part of teaching is to nurture. Students need to be encouraged to take risks and to grow in a learning environment where they feel safe. Susan understood that the love of learning is cultivated through encouragement, not fear.

As the year went on, Susan successfully ran a structured but creative classroom.

Keeping a good balance in your classroom can be a challenge. Let your students get to know you as fun and fair—but never as someone to fear.

Rule with mercy and grace, and your reward will be great.

"Creative minds always have been known
to survive any kind of bad training."
— Anna Freud

Einstein

Young Einstein was never considered a brilliant
child. Intellectually, he even seemed backward. He
learned to talk late. Little or none of his future
ability was detected in early childhood.

By age ten, he was considered precocious, but
in attitude only.

Even in high school, he was only considered
average at physics and mathematics. It wasn't until
Hermann Minkowski mentored him that his genius
was recognized.

After that, things began to change for Einstein.
His independence and self-confidence grew, so

much so that it was difficult for any university in the 1890s to satisfy him.

His spark of genius became fully ignited when he got a job in the patent office. Suddenly he saw the physical insights interwoven with the heavy machinery in the patent shop. It was there that Einstein's mathematical genius took flight. And history took one of its biggest leaps.

How often does genius fall through the cracks of the school system? Our challenge as teachers is to find creative ways to nurture independent thinkers and creative souls, encouraging them to reach beyond their imaginations.

Is there someone in your class today that could be, like Einstein, a diamond in the rough?

Provide for the gift of understanding and encouragement. You never know what gifts you'll allow to emerge!

"Be sure you put your feet in the right place, then stand firm."
— Abraham Lincoln

Pass or Fail?

Stan taught social studies at Melham Middle School for fifteen years and had the reputation of bringing history alive for his students. His students always seemed to thrive and do very well.

But each year he discovered more and more students lacking in basic reading skills, hindering essential comprehension.

"How did they get this far?" he questioned.

Two days before final grades were due, Stan had a conference with the principal. It seemed that two boys were failing not only his class, but every other class they were taking. The principal asked if

Stan could see his way clear to pass them.

This seemed stronger than a request, it seemed an expectation.

"I can't do that," Stan said. "They didn't pass. They didn't come to class. In fact, they did nothing!"

His principal still pressed. "They are too old. We need to pass them."

"Then someone else will have to pass them," rebutted Stan. "It's not fair to them or to the other students who worked so hard."

Although another teacher decided to give the boys a passing grade, Stan knew that he had done the right thing.

You may someday have to be the teacher who cares enough about the future of your students to keep them at the same level until they really learn.

There will be times when you must stand on principle, even when it is unpopular.

"If you judge people, you have
no time to love them."
— Mother Teresa

Soggy Leaves

by Tony Horning

Jamie came to school one morning with a
rolled-up towel that secured his priceless treasure.
Waiting to share was frustrating for both Jamie and
Mr. Taylor. This little boy, eager to share his
discovery, interrupted lesson after lesson.

When Jamie's time finally came, the students
formed a circle on the floor. Jamie lowered his
towel to the floor with such care and slowly
unrolled it to reveal a handful of old, soggy, brown
leaves from his yard—not the beautiful and
colorful leaves of autumn with their vibrant reds
and yellows; just plain, old, brown leaves.

As Mr. Taylor looked around that circle, he was surprised to see on the children's faces amazement, wonder, and joy!

Listening to the class you would have thought they were staring into the Grand Canyon. Captivated, these children held those soggy leaves as if they were newborn kittens.

There in that circle, the teacher became the student. For a brief moment, Mr. Taylor could remember a time when the simplest things in life brought wonder and joy to him as well.

Take time in your classroom to enjoy the simple pleasures.

If you miss the little things, you miss the vast majority of life.

"If a child lives with praise,
he learns to appreciate."
— Dorothy Nolte

Listen and Learn

Mary eagerly looked into the faces of her first class, fully expecting they'd look at her just as eagerly in return. However, eye contact wasn't easy to come by, and the only eagerness she saw was when they looked at the clock.

How do you compete with a clock? she thought.

Coming in behind another teacher in the middle of the year was hard enough. But coming behind a teacher who had been overly harsh made the situation even more complex.

Mary wondered if she would ever get past the wall that seemed so great between them. Their level of frustration, though unspoken, was immense. Her search for wisdom had only taken her to textbooks and research studies, but she did not find answers there.

One night, as she was unable to silence her thoughts in order to sleep—she made a decision that she needed to stop trying to fix her students and, instead, start trying to understand them.

She began to encourage her students in what seemed at times the smallest achievements, and invested much more time listening. By building up her students in their gifts and hearing them out on things, she created an amazing bond with them.

Even in her inexperience, she was able to find a connection with her students by simply showing how much she really cared.

What extra step can you take to connect with your students?

> Take the extra time to get to know your students and show you care.

"Leave as little to chance as possible.
Preparation is the key to success."
— Paul Brown

The Best Laid Plans

Miss Sanders had worked all summer devising a myriad of plans she hoped would capture and delight her very first kindergarten class.

With wide eyes, her first students anxiously surveyed the classroom. They saw storytelling murals, expressive mobiles, and activity centers peeking out of every corner!

Miss Sanders told the children they could investigate any part of the room they wanted.

Billy couldn't even find a place to begin. He began to wander from station to station becoming more confounded by the minute. Miss Sanders didn't notice the lone explorer whose frustration was building. Finally, in desperation, Billy stood mid-room and bellowed in protest.

Miss Sanders rushed to calm Billy but was suddenly surprised by another tearful voice from the opposite side of the room. There began a growing whir of little people overwhelmed by their new surroundings—missing their mothers. Within seconds, the class exploded into a chorus of crying.

Neighboring teachers rushed into the chaos and calmly helped Miss Sanders round up and comfort the overwhelmed kindergartners. In moments, all was well again.

Miss Sanders was grateful for the others with more experience who came to her rescue that day.

If you are a new teacher, don't be afraid to ask questions or glean from the wisdom of seasoned teachers.

Look to the experience of others who have gone before you. They are there to offer comfort as well as guidance.

"Little by little does the trick."
— Abraham Lincoln

Give It Time

by Ailene Doherty

Amy was an enthusiastic and optimistic first grade teacher. By Thanksgiving her students were progressing even faster than she had hoped—all except for Jonathan.

Jonathan seemed so withdrawn. Amy wondered what she could do to make the classroom a happier experience for him. Maybe she could move his seat near children who would encourage him. Maybe she could offer him some sort of reward or assign him a mentor.

Then she was hit by a thought. Maybe she was trying too hard to change Jonathan. Perhaps he just needed time and patience. Amy relaxed and decided to give him room to progress at his own pace.

Only a few weeks later, Jonathan came during recess and handed her a book, "This is my favorite book. Would you like to read some of it to the class?"

An amazing improvement. His first step. Ever so slowly, the changes took place and by the end of the year, Jonathan was voted as the student who made the most progress!

There will always be students who take longer to adjust and fit in. Some times all they really need is time, patience, and to know you are available if needed.

It takes some children longer than others to rise to the occasion. Remember to give them time and not rush to fix a problem that may adjust itself.

43

All communities have a culture.
It is the climate of their civilization.

— Walter Lippmann

Environment

Laura is a teacher who is very self-confident and, to be honest, has a good right to be. She has a knack for accurately assessing situations. Unfortunately, her timing isn't always right, and she often runs into resistance.

This year when Laura started at a new school, she was excited and very much at ease even though it had been five years since she'd stepped foot into a classroom. Her enthusiasm and creativity spirited her to take on new activities and programs.

Laura was used to spearheading new ideas, but she wasn't used to a principal who was resistant to that kind of energy. She was stopped at every turn. Anything new was shot down. Her principal was comfortable with the status quo—no more and no less.

Laura's innovation had been squelched and her bitterness grew. Frustrated, she decided that this school was not where she belonged and impulsively put in for a transfer for the next year.

Even though it is a principal's job to get to know his teachers, it is just as crucial for a new teacher to take time to get to know the culture of his school. What is valued? What are the rules? Who has the power?

Being watchful, learning, and working within the parameters of your school's environment helps ensure your ability to make changes and adjustments later, when it really counts.

Learn your school's culture; adapt and become part of the mold before you try to break it.

"By learning you will teach;
by teaching you will learn."
— Latin proverb

Teachers are Students

As teachers, we are perpetual students. Yes, we may take another college course here or there to renew our certificates, but we also learn from our own teaching experiences.

Through the act of teaching, we learn how to resolve conflicts effectively. We discover how to talk so others will listen. We remember what it's like to be a student, so we tread with care.

Remember the first time you had to teach fractions and it wasn't until the end of the lesson that you finally grasped it yourself? That's not something to worry about; that's something to celebrate!

Experiencing the learning process along with your students provides you with wonderful insight.

Tell your students—they will know they've really learned something when they can teach it to someone else. Give them opportunities within the classroom to teach.

To educate is to be a part of a cycle of learning and teaching.

When you attend an eye-opening workshop, teach others what you have learned. When you make a mistake, encourage others not to do the same.

Have a humble heart when it comes to this business of teaching. You never know what you might learn or from whom you might learn it.

Don't be afraid to become a student of your students.

"Education is not the filling of a pail,
but the lighting of a fire."
— William Butler Yeats

Light a Fire

With the new standardized test of basic skills in place, teachers scrambled to stay on top of their curricula so their students would perform well on the test. The demands were great, and the time was quite limited. They found themselves teaching around the test—not the preferred way to teach, but it seemed to be a necessary evil.

Ken, a math teacher, was worried about a group of students who were falling behind. He had only six more weeks to complete multiplication, yet some students were still struggling with the beginning concepts. What could he do?

The time needed to go back and re-teach these

48

few just wasn't there. But Ken was not willing to accept the idea that some students must fall through the cracks, either.

He realized, just as King Solomon centuries ago, that knowledge for knowledge's sake is meaningless. He decided to focus his attention on inspiring his students with a passion for learning. This inspiration would reach far beyond any one test; it would prepare them for the test of life.

With this goal, he made the best use of the time he had. By adding enthusiasm, props, and visuals to his teaching during those last few weeks, he inspired a combustible hunger for knowledge within his students.

It's the fire you light under your students that matters. It filters through the cracks and reaches students at every level.

The fire you light in your students for learning will affect them for a lifetime.

"See everything; overlook a great deal;
correct a little."
— Pope John XXIII

Discipline

Discipline is probably the most talked about
and most misunderstand aspect of education.
Discipline comes from the Latin *disciplino,* which
means *to instruct.* It's rooted in the idea of learning,
not punishment.

Formulating a discipline plan is the first thing
every teacher is expected to do, even before
writing lesson plans. Each teacher has different
discipline boundaries. And your discipline plan
may be very original.

The process of adjusting to various discipline
plans helps children learn how to adjust to the
differing expectations of people.

Too much discipline can frustrate the learner. You are not called to frustrate or nit-pick. Devise rules that are simple, easy to observe, and fair.

The more rules you have, the more rules you must keep track of! And if you're not careful, you'll end up spending most of your time catching kids in their mistakes.

Choose instead definable boundaries, and become an overseer instead of a bounty hunter. Correct only when absolutely necessary, and make sure you follow through on every consequence.

Utilize natural consequences whenever possible. For example, if a child does not study for his test, he will fail. Natural consequences are easily understood and enforced. More importantly, they teach life-lessons which will be essential and valuable to students later on.

Good teachers pick their battles rather than picking on students.

"Don't limit a child to your own learning,
for he was born in another time."
— Rabbinical saying

Inclusion

Jan waited patiently as her department head
worked his way through the team meeting agenda.
It was the second time she had been scheduled to
speak, but she had the sinking feeling they
wouldn't get to her this time either.

Jan's learning-disabled students were struggling
in the regular classroom environment—not
because of their ability, but because there was a
definite feeling of exclusion.

Jan needed to address this issue as an advocate
for her students. After all, who else would speak
up for them. Jan was willing to do whatever it
took to change the way the needs of her students

were perceived, but unless the team gave her a chance to talk, she wouldn't be able to make that needed difference.

Finally, it was her turn. Jan stuck to the facts, but not without emotion. Revealing her compassionate heart, Jan demonstrated to the other teachers what it was like to sit in a class where they were ignored, everything sounded garbled, and looked like nonsense.

As she made her final statement and returned to her seat, her team looked at her as if they had seen her for the first time. They were finally able to understand the helplessness her students felt.

Never allow an opportunity pass where you might be able to be an advocate for your students.

Remember that you speak for your students. Silence can be seen as agreement.

"They know enough
who know how to learn."
— Henry Adams

How to Learn

It wasn't until graduate school that Char learned how to learn. So much of her time in school had been spent memorizing meaningless facts. But in grad school Char learned how to think critically, synthesize information, and draw her own conclusions. She examined how she learned best and could identify different teaching styles easily. With this knowledge, all she had to do to succeed was to adjust her style when necessary.

Why does it take until graduate school before students learn how to learn, or better yet, how *they* learn?

Children have the capacity even as

kindergartners to recognize their own learning styles if they are shown how. Give your students the ability to discover their own learning styles, and their opportunities will be boundless. That awareness alone is power packed!

If you haven't taken a look at your own thinking and learning styles, you will not be able to help your students gain that same understanding. Take a chance and look inside yourself. You'll be pleasantly surprised at whom you meet.

Re-evaluate your *teaching style* by reflecting on your own *learning style.*

"In the arsenal of truth, there is
no greater weapon than fact."
— Lyndon B. Johnson

Revealing the Truth

"Honey, we need to stop at the office supply store. I need some things for my classroom," Sue said to her husband.

"What do you need this time?" he asked.

"The usual. Copy paper, black and red pens, legal pads, and some file folders."

"Can't you just get them from the supply closet?" he asked.

"What supply closet?" Sue laughed. "Once we run out, we're out. And it's too much trouble to get the bookkeeper to make out a purchase order just for some pencils. It's quicker to buy them myself."

When surveyed, teachers said they spend anywhere between $200 to $2,000 per year on supplies for their classroom. Teachers are accustomed to filling in the gaps. Sometimes teachers must even supply the basics.

Unfortunately, spending our own money can hinder the cause of teachers more than it helps. The budget crunch is not felt by key decision makers when teachers spend their own money trying to fix the problem themselves.

Try to remember, when tempted to supplement your classroom from your own funds, that your generosity may be masking budget insufficiencies that so desperately need to be revealed. Although it can be very inconvenient and frustrating, going through the wait or a little red tape reveals the need so things can be changed.

Sometimes it's better to do without in order to highlight a problem to parents and administrators.

"I can live for two months
on a good compliment."
— Mark Twain

Compliment
by Ailene Doherty

Dr. McGuire was principal at Lackspoor High School. He was, undoubtedly, the most efficient person the teachers had ever worked with. He was, however, one of the most frustrating administrators on the staff. He never complimented them, neither did he criticize. He just issued bulletins stating what should happen and when.

After Alicia had been in the system for many years, she learned that Dr. McGuire's wife was very ill. She knew a sentimental card would not be appropriate to send to him. So she decided to bake her culinary specialty, an angel food cake, and give it to him. If he didn't approve of such a gesture, she couldn't be too severely punished, for she already had tenure!

Alicia's delight was unbounded the next day when Dr. McGuire handed her a ragged piece of a brown paper bag on which he had written a note that read, "You are not only a good cook, but a very good teacher."

Alicia went to her classroom, clutching her first compliment from her principal, marveling at the power of that small act of kindness.

The power of a genuine compliment is never wasted and is the best investment you can make in those around you.

Invest in your students, show your belief in them, compliment them, and acknowledge their gifts.

"Nothing in the world can
take the place of persistence."
— Calvin Coolidge

Perseverance

by Ailene Doherty

Jenny's tenth graders loved *Shane,* the little
novel by Jack Schaefer. And this novel became a
tradition she shared every year.

Two of the main characters are Joe and Marian
Starrett, homesteaders in Wyoming in the 1880s.
Joe labored diligently to clear their land. Day after
day he tried to uproot an old stump, wondering
whether he would ever conquer it. But one day his
perseverance paid off, and the stubborn old stump
rolled to his feet. Marian was just as determined as
her husband.

On one occasion, she forgot about an apple pie

she had put in the oven. That pie was ruined, but without hesitation she baked another one.

Jenny had learned many a lesson from Joe and Marian. Sometimes, when she had worked for hours on bulletin boards at school and still didn't feel satisfied, she would say to herself, "Keep at it; Marian did."

Many mornings, Jenny arrived at school early to help pupils with their essay writing. She became disheartened sometimes because a student who was an electronic whiz still found it difficult to express thoughts on paper.

But she kept trying and usually had the thrill of conquering her own kind of stubborn stump.

Stick it out with your students; there is no greater reward than to see a student finally break through and triumph!

If you give up, you give up on your students. They deserve your perseverance.

"If you want to be a leader with a
large following, just obey the speed limit
on a winding two-lane road."
— Charles Farr

Walk in Line

When Flora walked her class down the hallway
toward the lunchroom each day, she was
determined to teach them how to walk straight,
tall, and with purpose in mind. She didn't want
them wandering aimlessly down the corridor.

Flora expected her kindergartners to learn the
right way to do things, and learning how to walk
together in line was their first opportunity to do so.

When older classes would walk down the hall
opposite her class and were rowdy and misdirected,
she would point it out to her students. "See that

class? Let's show them the right way to walk respectfully." Her students would proudly stand to attention, passing the older class with quiet sophistication.

New students to her class would be indoctrinated in line-walking their very first day. Flora would say, "Let me show you how it's done." And then she would walk forward leading her class like a mother duck leading her focused ducklings. Her students caught on quickly. It was truly a thing of grace and beauty.

Teachers are leaders. Lead your students on the right path by showing them what you want and how you want it done. Leading your students in the way that they should go begins with the simplest of tasks.

Let them see how *you* walk.

> The way you travel through life is the most powerful legacy you can give your students.

"Motivation is when your dreams
put on work clothes."
— Parkes Robinson

Dreams

Lori could never understand the mentality
some of her contemporaries had when it came to
fulfilling their dreams. They believed that the
dream itself was enough. Lori was baffled at the
"someday I'll be discovered" attitude.

She had dreams, too. Lori dreamed that she
would become a teacher. So she put herself through
college. She dreamed that she would someday teach
teachers, so she got her Ph.D. She dreamed of
writing books, so she learned how, began speaking
at educational conferences, and was published!

Lori believed that dreams shouldn't just remain
dreams; they should become reality—knowing that

there may be those dreams that will always be dreams.

Lori also has a dream to travel abroad and be a missionary teacher, or to start her own school in the states. And as far-fetched and unreachable as that may seem to her now, it is attainable. It just means work and time.

What are your dreams?

If you think you've put aside your dreams, think again.

"I make progress by having people around
me who are smarter than I am—
and listening to them."
— Harry J. Kaiser

The Team

Upon becoming an administrator, Madelyn felt
overwhelmed. Although she had trained for this
position and had all the right degrees behind her,
she knew there was more to it than that. She had
to depend on the counsel of those already there.

The trick was figuring out on whom she could
depend. After a few months of getting to know her
staff, she knew it was not really "her" staff. They
were still quite attached to her predecessor.

This arrangement could have hindered the
overall progress of the department. Madelyn

couldn't be the expert in everything. Curriculum was her strength, but scheduling was not. Parent interaction was something she reveled in, but a public image was not. She needed people who could fill in the gaps and make the team whole. Though at times uneasy, she had to depend on the strengths of her team.

As opportunities arose, either out of resignations or transfers, Madelyn's mission was to scout out experts.

By the end of the second year, she felt like she finally had a dynamic team of players in her department and found it easy to defer to their judgment. It became evident that leading where she was strong was expected and preferred by all those involved.

Even if you can't hand pick your staff, rely on the best of their abilities. When they shine, the team shines.

"You've got to continue to grow or
you're just like last night's cornbread—
stale and dry."
— Loretta Lynn

Spice It Up!

Are you in a teaching rut? How do you know?

Can you teach that algebra lesson in your
sleep? Be careful—you might be teaching while
your students sleep!

Strive to be a "seasoned" teacher—one who
doesn't lack vigor. A seasoned teacher is one who
brings variety, zip, and delight into the classroom.

Something that is seasoned wakes up the taste
buds and tempts the recipient to want more. Once
tasted, it is craved!

Do your students get excited by your teaching?

Do they want more?

How can you become seasoned instead of growing stale? What can you add to your repertoire that is unusual and interesting? How can you be surprising and tantalizing? You don't have to be a sideshow. You just need to bring your teaching back to life.

All around you are opportunities to do things differently. Send away for that catalog. Enroll in that class. Go listen to that speaker. Find your own personal zest!

Not only will your students be coming back for more, but you will enjoy your own teaching again.

Spice up your teaching. Bring a new excitement into your classroom.

"When you make a mistake, admit it;
learn from it and don't repeat it."
— Bear Bryant

Learn from Mistakes

Natalie's previous principals had trained her to be a good teacher—one who accepted responsibility willingly and expertly.

Her move to the district office was one she welcomed and believed was the next step for her. Although she missed the classroom, she felt she'd be able to make a difference higher up.

Her first assignment as a resource teacher was to track down a missing camcorder reported stolen from a local high school. Natalie felt confident in her new position and, since the school's assistant principal was a former colleague, felt quite comfortable approaching him with this situation.

Unfortunately, as she began to question the assistant principal's handling of the robbery, her confidence was perceived as intimidation. She not only met resistance, but she also alienated the one person who could have given her answers.

Realizing her mistake she tried to apologize, but instead of seeming genuine, she came across as unprofessional. A complaint was filed, and Natalie was demoted to desk work the very next day.

Natalie jumped rashly into a role she thought had inherent power and respect. The truth is that power and respect are earned, not bestowed by virtue of the position.

When you are in a new situation, give yourself some time to learn the ropes and your decision making will be much more effective.

Take the time to learn the culture of your new environment before you act.

"It is sheer waste of time to imagine what I
would do if things were different.
They are not different."
— Dr. Frank Crane

Reproof

Bob just couldn't get comfortable in his school
environment. There were so many things he
wished were different. To add to this he was the
only male teacher on his team.

If there were more men here, he thought, *maybe
I'd feel more a part of things.* He had been a math
major in college and went into teaching as an
afterthought. It was not his original intention, and
he was uncertain in his teaching role.

Constantly he analyzed his situation for things
that could have been done differently. And his

colleagues tired of his constant deliberating on the matter.

Most of the time, the other teachers just quietly ate their lunch as Bob complained. One day Bob muttered, "If only things were different. . . ."

Finally, one of his friends spoke up and said, "But they aren't different. Get over it, and go on!"

Bob looked stunned, just as if he had been slapped across the face. After a moment, his face softened and he realized his friend was right. It was that very statement that enabled Bob to transform his perspective, move on, and enjoy his position as a teacher.

Hearing the truth can be painful, but try to remember a friend's reproof is rooted in love and can be an opportunity for change.

Things can be different only if you can make them different.

"If you don't like the road you're walking,
start paving another one."
— Dolly Parton

The Right Path

Patricia's mother was a teacher. Her grandmother was a teacher. Both of her sisters were teachers. Yet her mother encouraged her to do something else. She said, "You can do better."

To appease her mother, Patricia became a speech pathologist. She graduated with honors and went to work in a notable hospital for children.

After three years with different clients every hour and an environment she was uncomfortable in, she found herself dreading the start of each new day.

The symptoms of dissatisfaction surfaced. Patricia began to be chronically late. She withdrew socially at the hospital. She was tired all the time and began to hate the career path she had chosen.

One day, one of her young clients was about to be dismissed from her care. The parents asked Patricia if she would accompany them to a school meeting and explain their son's speech difficulties to the speech teacher there.

Patricia went willingly. She had always been curious about the school setting. After their meeting, she wandered the school soaking up its atmosphere thinking, *This is where I belong!*

The very next day, Patricia took immediate steps toward moving her career into the school system. For the first time in her life, she was content and fulfilled in her work. She had accomplished her own dream . . . she had followed her own heart.

Have you chosen your own path?

Have you followed your own heart's desires?

> Make sure you choose your own path, and stick to it.

"A good deed is never lost;
he who sows courtesy reaps friendship,
and he who plants kindness gathers love."

— St. Basil

George Washington Carver

Whenever George Washington Carver tried to attend a school, he was quickly either turned away or ridiculed because he was black.

Following the Civil War, it wasn't easy for former slaves to carve out a life for themselves. Even so, George pressed on.

The Listons were a white couple whom George befriended while at Simpson College in Iowa. They owned a bookstore, and he spent most of his free time there. Later George chose to attend Iowa State, and once again he was the only black student. Immediately, he was the object of racial insults. In a letter to the Listons, Carver complained about the way he was being treated.

Mrs. Liston took the train to Iowa State and walked the entire campus on his arm. "The next day everything was different," Carver later explained. "The ice was broken, and from then on, things went very much easier."

Students who don't quite fit in for one reason or another sometimes just need a helping hand—not necessarily to help them reach but to help them connect.

Is there a student in your midst who could use your endorsement today?

Be an advocate for someone who really needs it.

"What is honored in a country
will be cultivated there."
— Plato

What Does Your Garden Grow?

Each school has its own unique culture.

A small school will look and function differently from a large school. An inner city school will look dramatically different from a rural or suburban school. Elementary is different from secondary; private is different from public.

Where the differences lie are not just in the structures themselves, but in the values and beliefs of the inhabitants.

Look deep into a school, and you can see what is cherished. Walk the halls, and you will see what they value.

Walk into a school that looks sterile with white blank walls, no signage, and complete silence, and you will feel like you have walked into a hospital. This school's leaders believe that students are there to be cured by their teaching.

Walk into another school with colorful walls, covered with students' artwork—where teachers' doors are adorned with their personal style, and you will see a school that values students' creations and teachers' personalities. It is a welcoming atmosphere, one that fosters growth.

Where do creative minds prefer to flower? They prefer a place where there is light, warmth, and plenty of food.

Is your school a place for growth? It could be! Begin with your classroom.

Decide today to be a tiller of the soil in your school.

"The secret of success is
constancy to purpose."
— Benjamin Disraeli

The Main Thing
by Tony Horning

As a student teacher, Carl was thrilled with all
of the fun and innovative things he had the
opportunity to introduce to his students.
Unbeknownst to him, his supervising teachers
were taking care of the plethora of other duties,
leaving him with a false perception of freedom as a
teacher. Before he realized it, he had given in to the
routine and lost touch of his sense of purpose.

As a new teacher, it isn't long before innovation
is traded for familiarity. Many a college graduate
enters their first classroom, finding there is far more
awaiting them than they could have ever imagined.

They discover themselves under an avalanche of paperwork from students, the principal, and the district. Creativity and enthusiasm can easily be squelched by the overwhelming and unseen demands of the classroom.

Eventually Carl realized his dissipation. He knew assigning and grading work wasn't teaching. He refocused his attention and developed healthy boundaries for himself, his students, and the daily pressing requirements. As a result, the flashes of brilliance and creativity once again entered his classroom. His students flourished and teaching again became his rediscovered passion.

More than anything else, students need you to be a leader who is able to reinforce the fact that they are worth more than all the homework you could ever assign.

Remember, the main thing is to keep the main thing the main thing.

"A true leader always keeps an element
of surprise up his sleeve, which others
cannot grasp but which keeps his
public excited and breathless."
— Charles de Gaulle

Open House

Tess inspected her room one final time before
the parents arrived.

Students' work assignments were prominently
displayed, and volunteer sign-up sheets were in
plain view. The room looked both organized and
creative. This was Tess's tenth open house night,
but she still got butterflies as parents took their
seats at the children's desks. She felt more on
display than her students' creations.

This was her chance to make a good first

impression. It might be one of the only times she would see these parents face-to-face. She wanted it to be a positive experience—one that instilled trust and confidence in her ability to teach their children.

The room was packed—standing room only. Tess circulated the crowd, handing out a scavenger hunt she thought might break the ice. Within minutes children and parents were navigating the room looking for the places and things on her list. When at last everyone returned to their seats, Tess relaxed as she saw the smiling, excited faces.

It was a good start to a great year.

Putting forth the extra effort necessary to make parents feel confident about your teaching will produce enduring rewards.

Each year, show yourself to the parents as capable. Parents like to know that you are in charge!

"No act of kindness, no matter
how small, is ever wasted."
— Aesop

Conferences

Conducting a parent-teacher conference wasn't covered in Sarah's education courses. Once a teacher, she found that she was expected to meet with each parent at least once a year.

Most of her students were doing exceptionally well, with good grades and good behavior. But there were a few who were frustrating. She was dreading their conferences.

She started with easier conferences first, secretly hoping that the parents of the more difficult students wouldn't even show up.

After two or three conferences, Sarah noticed that once she conveyed the positive things about her students, parents responded with, "Please don't hesitate to let us know if Johnny ever strays." And Sarah wondered if the same might happen with the parents she was avoiding.

She called each of the parents of her most challenging students and told them at least one positive thing about their child. It wasn't easy, but it did force her to concentrate on the strengths of these students.

A few weeks later she scheduled their conferences. She repeated the positives and then enlisted help with the negative. She was encouraged to discover that these parents were just as willing to help and assured her that they would be supportive.

Not all of your challenges will be as easily solved. But remaining positive opens the door for parents to work with you toward solutions.

> Tell parents the positive first. It makes the negative more palatable later.

"It takes seventy-two muscles to frown,
but only thirteen to smile."
— Anonymous

WYSIWYG

Sometimes the demands on teachers can be quite stressful.

In one day, you might be expected to fill out a mountain of paperwork, calm a tense parent, meet with your team about next year's budget, and . . . oh yes . . . teach!

The pressure of these demands can make it difficult to face the wide-eyed wonder in your students with enthusiasm day after day.

Your countenance speaks volumes. If your eyes are downcast or you stare with indifference when you teach, you cannot convey a love for learning to your students. But what if you just don't feel especially excited about vocabulary that day?

Scientists have found that even forced laughter has a beneficial effect, both mentally and physically. You may think that "faking it" is hypocritical, but sometimes in the midst of that forced smile, you actually do smile. A simple smile can change your attitude and recharge your teaching.

Don't forget "WYSIWYG": What You See Is What You Get. What are your students "getting" from you today?

Next time you feel nervous, tired, or stressed, indulge in a good laugh.

"If there be any truer measure of
a man than by what he does,
it must be by what he gives."
— Robert South

New Teacher

Jami was the newest teacher at Jackson Elementary.

Walking into the teachers' lounge her first day, she felt very much like an outsider. She sat at a table alone and unpacked her lunch. Within a few minutes the tables filled, and the room buzzed with discussions of kids, plans, and happenings of the day.

No one seemed to notice Jami.

Halfway through lunch, the principal walked in to notify another teacher of a phone call. She called to Jami before she breezed out the door, "Glad to have you with us, Miss Smith." Jami immediately felt more welcome and finally visible.

"Who are you substituting for today, dear?" a seasoned teacher asked.

"Oh, no. I'm a teacher here. I'm the new reading specialist," Jami said.

Suddenly, she was not only visible but on display. Those at her table seemed genuinely interested in her, asking her questions about her background and her thoughts on teaching.

How do you welcome a new teacher? When a new teacher arrives, assert yourself to do those things for others which would have made you feel more comfortable.

Try to remember how it felt when you were the new teacher.

If you're a seasoned teacher, take steps to make new teachers feel welcome.

"Don't find fault. Find a remedy."
— Henry Ford

Protective Parents

On first impression, Mrs. Gladstone was the parent most teachers dream of. She volunteered in the classroom two mornings a week. She was a partner in her daughter's learning.

However, as the year progressed, Mrs. Gladstone's involvement became overwhelming.

She started calling the teacher at home on the weekends. She was at her daughter's side for every field trip, whether she was needed or not. She began showing up for lunch every day.

While the teacher appreciated Mrs. Gladstone's intentions, she could tell Natalie was uncomfortable with her mother's constant presence.

The teacher tried to dissuade Mrs. Gladstone from coming on field trips and encouraged her to cut lunch dates down a bit. Mrs. Gladstone nervously refused the advice. She wasn't ready to let go.

Rather than causing unnecessary tension which could potentially damage the teacher-parent relationship, this teacher decided to change her strategy, including Natalie in group activities when her mother wasn't there. It took extra effort but in the end it was a win/win situation benefiting everyone.

In dealing with potential parental conflict, remember some of the best results can be derived from compromise.

Be gracious and understanding in dealing with parents, keeping in mind that they are entrusting you with their most treasured gifts.

"It takes time to save time."
— Joe Taylor

Be Prepared

Lesson plans are just that—plans. They don't just appear! Yet there are times when all teachers feel they don't have time to write down strategic plans.

Do you know teachers who "fly by the seat of their pants"—who always seem to be rushing around to gather materials at the last minute and aren't quite sure what page they are on until the kids tell them?

Granted there are too many things teachers have to do that have nothing to do with teaching. No one likes to bring work home. And a teacher's time is a precious commodity.

But the time spent trying to decide, *What are we going to do today?* is not yours. It's your students'.

Modeling time management and efficiency is an important part of the teaching process.

Your principal, fellow teachers, students, and your students' parents all watch how you manage your time. Your time management showcases your values and speaks your priorities.

What are you spending your time on today? How much time are you investing into those things or people that matter to you most?

Show your students that they matter to you. Come to class prepared!

"Blessed are they who heal us of
self-despisings. Of all services
which can be done to man,
I know of none more precious."
—William Hale White

Vocalist

Beth was considered the top vocalist in the choir.

The year had been hectic, and she didn't put her normal preparation into a difficult piece she was to perform for a major competition. Her life as a senior was incredibly busy, and she just didn't devote the time she needed in practice.

When her time came to perform, she forgot some of the words and didn't receive her usual high rating.

Beth felt awful.

Beth's choir director offered words of consolation on the bus on their way home. Those words only seemed to intensify the guilt she felt. She not only let herself down, but felt she had let her school down.

After the others got off the bus, Beth burst into tears. She sobbed with her head down, knowing she had not done her best. She felt a hand on her back and looked up to see her director with big tears in his eyes, too.

His tears brought healing to Beth's heart.

She knew by his words that he believed she could do better next time, but she knew by his heartfelt concern that he would be there to help her.

More than any other thing, your heartfelt and compassionate acts toward your students will lift defeated hearts.

Reveal your heart, and heal a soul.

"The heart benevolent and kind . . .
most resembles God."
— Robert Burns

Leo Buscaglia

Best-selling author Leo Buscaglia grew up in an Italian home. He actually learned English as a second language. Upon entering school, Leo was branded as mentally deficient, and recommended to be placed in a special class. He was "written off" by those who believed to know better.

Miss Hunt taught this special class. She was caring, warm, and paid little attention to the labels placed on her students. Miss Hunt modeled a love of learning to all in her class and saw Leo as rich in potential.

In Miss Hunt's class, Buscaglia blossomed, and after several months, Miss Hunt insisted he be re-tested. The results placed him into the regular classroom system.

Miss Hunt's door was always open to Buscaglia. She encouraged him and convinced him that wonderful things were in store.

Do you know a child who has been "written off" or "lost in the shuffle," by parents, teachers, or other students?

Perhaps you are the teacher, like Miss Hunt, who will give him or her the benefit of doubt.

A heart of compassion and belief can be the very thing that causes a student to "make it."

"An idea is salvation by imagination."
— Frank Lloyd Wright

Yelling

Susan's high expectations for her students sometimes led to some frustrating moments. She taught seventh grade, and found she was raising her voice frequently just to get their attention. Susan hated to yell. It wasn't in her nature, and it was extremely frustrating. Although it had some shock value, mostly it just gave her a sore throat.

Susan needed a better way to get her students' attention—something that would do the job without the stress. She always thought she had good control of her class. Now she wasn't quite sure. There had to be a better way.

Later that week she attended a workshop with

200 hundred other teachers. Many of the teachers hadn't seen each other in quite some time, and the initial visiting created quite a commotion.

The leader, impervious to the noise, announced in a normal voice, "If you can hear my voice, clap twice."

Then as the clamor decreased, "If you can hear my voice, clap three times." Suddenly the room was quiet.

That simple demonstration of control was exactly what Susan was looking for. She couldn't wait to begin applying it to her own classes that very next week.

Open your imagination to new and creative measures to capture the attention of your class.

Learn to diffuse frustrations by placing your energies into seeking positive, active solutions.

"Silence is not always tact . . .
it is tact that is golden, not silence."
— Samuel Butler

Gossip

Gossip can abound in a teachers' lounge.

If not careful, teachers can get caught up in scrutinizing each other's style, demeanor, or appearance.

Chad decided a long time ago that he would not engage in any deliberate attempt to slander a fellow teacher. Even so, he became an unwilling participant in some very destructive gossip. To the other teachers, his silence meant agreement.

He found out later that he had been maligned as well.

Chad was hurt and disappointed. He painfully

realized how loud his silence was heard and how misunderstood its meaning was. Plans for damage control raced through his mind as he chased vindication. What could he say? What could he do?

He needed words—but not words that declared his innocence—words of peace. Chad determined that day to use only words that would uplift and edify his colleagues. He decided to defuse them with kindness.

By resolving to disengage from the circles of gossip and speak kind words instead, you will win the respect of your colleagues. More importantly you could ultimately change the environment and team spirit of your school leadership.

Others will find little to gossip about if you stay busy spreading cheer, showing empathy, and teaching well.

"Between whom there is hearty truth,
there is love."
— Henry David Thoreau

Unprofessional Behavior

Jessica was a new, young teacher whose enthusiasm sometimes was in need of a bridle.

Giving compliments came naturally to her and she showered them on her colleagues whenever the spirit moved her. Jessica was also a very physical person who many times hugged teachers she especially appreciated.

She was particularly appreciative of the way Mr. Blue, the gym teacher, treated her kindergartners. He was loved by the students, respected by the parents, and had a winsome personality. Mr. Blue was also a handsome, married man.

Jessica's endless hugs and enthusiasm, albeit

well-intended, lacked professional boundaries. And talk of Jessica's behavior gave rise to many assaults on her character. It also caused wondering whispers about Mr. Blue.

Concerned, a close colleague sat down with Jessica and gently addressed the situation before it injured her career. Not only did Jessica accept the advice from her colleague, she was most appreciative.

Should you find yourself in a similar situation, check your own motives. Ask yourself, *Do I really want to help this person?* and if so, try to:

1. do no harm.

2. be sensitive, not superior.

3. keep your emotions in check.

4. depersonalize the issue.

5. be brief.

Sometimes the best way to show a person you value them is to lovingly speak the truth.

> If your motive is really to help, you'll find a way to speak the truth in love.

"Education is helping the child
realize his potentialities."
— Erich Fromm

Jimmy

Jimmy challenged his teacher day after day.

The lesson was always interrupted to deal with some outburst or rule infraction. Mrs. Jenkins tried strict adherence to her discipline plan. She tried ignoring his behavior. She even tried bribing Jimmy. All these solutions were short-lived. They were Band-Aids when only holistic care would do.

As all teachers do, Mrs. Jenkins knew her students quite well. She knew Jimmy's likes and dislikes, strengths and weaknesses, gifts and talents. And she decided to try a combination approach that would address the whole child and not just his behavior.

Since Jimmy was artistic, Mrs. Jenkins gave him the responsibility of making posters. Since he worked better alone than in a group, she assigned him specific tasks at group times. And since he liked attention, she called on him for answers even before he could raise his hand.

In time, Jimmy's outbursts decreased. His productivity increased. Mrs. Jenkins had found a better way for Jimmy and for herself.

Try to always remember, your students are more than a set of behaviors. They are people who have needs, desires, and preferences. When problems arise, look past the situation and into the child.

Know your students well enough to identify what they need. Then give it to them.

Choose not to label your students by their behaviors. Help them evolve into something better than they thought they could be.

"Though we travel the world over to find the beautiful, we must carry it with us or we find it not."
— Ralph Waldo Emerson

Dolphin Watch

Eileen's commute to school each day exhausted her. It took her over two bridges and through horrendous morning traffic. By the time she finally reached her classroom, she was usually frazzled.

She tried leaving home earlier, but because of where she lived, that didn't make any difference. She still found herself sitting on these bridges for an inordinate amount of time.

One Monday morning there was an accident on the bridge. Eileen actually took the car out of gear this time to sit and wait. It was a breezy Florida morning and the stretch of beach along the approach to the bridge attracted morning walkers. *I wish I could leave my car behind and walk along the beach myself,* Eileen thought.

Suddenly people were getting out of their cars and pointing to the warm Florida waters. Eileen slid out the passenger's door to see what the commotion was. A pod of dolphins were slicing through the waters just offshore.

Eileen was flooded with a sense of wonder and peace.

From that day forward, she saw the slow traffic as a chance to dolphin watch! And that simple observation changed her life.

In the fast pace of life, take time to smell the roses.

Remember not to get so wrapped up in life that you miss the beauty that is around you.

"The highest reward for a man's
toil is not what he gets for it,
but what he becomes by it."
— Ruskin

Meetings

There are times when it seems that schools
have become more like a place for teachers to have
meetings, rather than teach.

School improvement meetings, technology
meetings, parent-teacher meetings, and community
involvement meetings are carried on across the
country. It's easy to view these meetings and
committees as one more thing you, as a busy
teacher, don't really have time for. Then when the
meetings are conducted outside school hours and
infringe on personal time, you might even feel
confined and become frustrated or indignant.

Yet, what does an indignant attitude communicate to administrators, parents, and other teachers? Although tempted to think otherwise, these meetings go on to create a better atmosphere for our students in which to learn.

Perhaps you think your schools are fine just the way they are.

Perhaps you might take a closer look.

All organizations can stand improvement. Do you help the process?

You know the right thing to do.

The question is, "Do you love your students enough to do it?"

Quality schools are the result of quality teachers going above and beyond the call of duty.

"No one is useless in the world who lightens the burden of it for anyone else."
— Charles Dickens

Encourage

Judith's decision to "job share" this year was rooted in her desire to stay at home with her newborn daughter, at least part of the time. This choice wasn't working out as smoothly as she had expected.

The baby seemed to be sick much of the time. Judith never had enough planning time, and teaming with her partner left much to be desired. Most days she came to work exhausted and close to tears.

It was a parent who finally noticed her anguish and discouragement. This parent offered more than just words of comfort; she offered friendship. You see, she had walked in those shoes herself.

Judith got through that year, due in great part to the understanding and encouragement of a caring parent.

Teachers everywhere know the benefits of being an encourager to their students.

Everyone needs someone to cheer for them now and then. Don't let the extent of your encouragement end with your students. Fellow teachers need encouragement, too.

Is there a teacher on your staff who could benefit from your encouragement today?

"You cannot shake hands
with a clenched fist."
— Indira Ghandi

Turnover

Last year Joy found herself to be the only first grade teacher left on her team after an unprecedented number of other teachers transferred. These empty first grade slots were filled by teachers from four different schools, each with a different background and agenda.

Their first team meeting was the first time they had been introduced to each other. Joy wondered if she should have transferred, too. Joy's apprehension was mirrored in the faces of all four of the other teachers. There was an uncomfortable silence as they sat across from each other at the child sized activity table.

After a few minutes of polite introductions, Joy decided to jump in with both feet. "This can be either a miserable experience, or it can be the best year any of us have ever had." The teachers began to open up and share, each committing to making it work together.

That year became the best they had ever experienced. It was the first year of four dynamic years together.

The diversity of the group actually became its strength. For example: One teacher's experiences were from an inner city school. She knew a lot about high risk kids. So when any of them came across that kind of child, she became the "expert" and helped them handle the situation.

When conflict came, they worked through it and became a stronger team together.

Don't panic when adversity comes. Embrace it and give it the chance to help you grow.

"Tact is the art of making a point
without making an enemy."
— Howard W. Newton

Accentuate the Positive

Carolyn wasn't quite sure when it all began. All she knew was that her tolerance for incompetence had diminished.

She was very concerned about one of her seventh grade science teachers. Mr. Roski's students were failing left and right. Students had reported that he typically sat at this desk reading the newspaper and looked up every so often to scowl at potential disrupters. He had become ineffective as a teacher and was so intense that even the parents were too intimidated to complain.

The bigger problem was that Mr. Roski had been at Jefferson Jr. High longer than anyone, including the administrators.

Carolyn knew that as principal, her actions, or lack thereof, would be testimony to her own effectiveness. She began to shine the light on those teachers who were doing exceptionally well. She even generated press releases to the local media about teachers and programs of which she was especially proud.

Parents began to request transfers into celebrated teachers' classes. This wave of positive energy didn't sweep Mr. Roski up—it swept him away. Actually, he jumped right off the boat and chose to retire early.

Many times it's more effective to accentuate the positives than it is to eliminate the negatives!

"Catch 'em being good" applies to both students and teachers.

"He . . . got the better of himself, and that's
the best kind of victory one can wish for."
— Miguel deCervantes

Sweet Spot

In baseball, players talk of the "sweet spot." They
describe it as hitting the ball in such a way that you
know instinctively it's going out of the park.

Many athletes can relate to the sweet spot.
Runners know when they run in the kind of
rhythm that will win the race. Swimmers feel
themselves slicing through the water toward
victory. Olympic Gold Medalists will tell you the
moment they knew they had won—way before
they crossed the finish line!

Likewise as a teacher, you know what it feels
like when a concept clicks. You see the lights go on
in students' eyes and the wheels begin to turn in

their brains. These are the lessons you allow to run over. These are the ones that even your most challenging students latch on to. These are the ones that make a lasting impact that your students will remember, even into adulthood. It's a feeling you crave to define your teaching.

It's not realistic to expect to teach in the "sweet spot" every time. Everyone has off days. But those athletes who know what it feels like, chase the security it provides.

What does it take?

It takes practice, commitment, and the desire to perform only at your best.

Decide today to do your best.

"Be a friend to thyself, and
others will be so too."
— Thomas Fuller

Birds of a Feather

Rob was accustomed to being the only male
teacher in his school and craved camaraderie with
teachers who were like-minded.

Sometimes there seemed to be too much
negativity in the teachers' lounge. He longed to
talk to teachers who looked at kids the way he did,
worked the way he did, and considered parents the
way he did.

During the past ten years, Rob had changed
schools four times in search of a faculty with his
same mindset. He began to wonder if he even
belonged in the teaching environment. He
considered going into another line of work, but he

knew he'd miss the kids too much.

Rob decided to stick it out and put all thoughts about transferring again out of his mind.

After three years he finally befriended a new teacher at this school. They thought and taught very much alike and their friendship was fun and invigorating. Over the next few years, Rob began to meet at least one teacher a year whom he could talk with and exchange new ideas.

These tiny morsels of collegiality were rewarding and expanded his vision for teaching.

Just as the rewards of teaching may be few and far between, so may be the teachers after your own heart. But they, like those rare rewards, will be a powerful influence in your life.

Reach out and get to know your colleagues. You may discover a kindred spirit.

"Give to every other human being
every right that you claim for yourself."
— Robert G. Ingersoll

Labels

Teachers know the damage that can be done when a child is labeled. That label can remain with the child for years to come.

Whether for failings and inadequacies or even talents and achievements, labels do harm. They hinder children from excelling and believing in themselves and can even place undo stress on a gifted child.

Educational labels aren't limited to students. We can also get caught up in labeling fellow teachers, parents, leadership, and administration.

It can be as subtle as "She's the beginning

teacher" or "That child has difficult parents."

Whether the labels are spoken or not, the damage is done. Reputations are challenged. Perceptions are defined.

Just as struggling students need to be seen as students first, teachers need to be seen as teachers first.

Perception is reality for each of us. If you view your fellow teacher as lazy, then that's the reality of the situation to you. If instead, you choose to view that person as a teacher who needs help staying motivated, you can now relate to him or her, and even help touch their life.

Decide today to challenge your own perceptions; you might really make a difference in another's life.

Labels belong on cans, not people. Can you find it within yourself to clarify your view of others?

"What comes from the heart,
goes to the heart."
— Samuel Taylor Coleridge

Support Staff

It takes a lot of people to make a school run. The staff includes teachers, administration, kitchen staff, custodians, building maintenance, and the list goes on.

If you are new to a school, introduce yourself first to these critical groups of workers.

This is not to say that there aren't kitchen workers who yell at the kids too much or head plant operators who disappear when there's work to be done. This is just to say that without them your job would be much more difficult.

The growing sizes of our schools dictate that

we hire more support staff. Just as you can't keep your car running without a mechanic and fuel, you need support staff to help bring to life all you aspire for your students.

Go out of your way to get to know the support staff at your school. Offer tokens of appreciation periodically. Speak kindly to and about these people. Offer words of encouragement and compliment them in front of others.

Your boards will always be cleaned, you'll be served an extra helping of your favorite lunch, and you will also build up relationships within your school. Most importantly you will be teaching your most valuable lesson to your students—respect for others.

Model for your students, respect for others and team spirit.

"No one can make you feel inferior
without your consent."
— Eleanor Roosevelt

Student or Teacher?

Sharon felt intimidated on her first day of internship.

At only twenty-one she was about to walk the halls of her rival high school from her own school days. Strangely enough, it felt all too familiar.

The huddled bodies outside the cafeteria. The frenzy of the first bell. The wooden desks all in a row in lecture style. She felt like a student standing there in the front office, her assignment in hand, waiting to see the principal.

After some quick introductions and a lackluster tour, Sharon hurried to her first class. Her pace quickened as she approached the main hallway.

Then, like a shot in the dark, she heard, "WALK!"

Sharon turned to apologize before entering the classroom. Then she thought to herself, *Hey, am I the teacher or the student?*

Later that day, she entered the teachers' lunchroom. As she navigated the ala carte line, she was abruptly stopped by a teacher whose voice she recognized from earlier that day.

"Young lady, what are you doing here? This is for teachers only."

"I'm not a student," Sharon replied, standing tall. "I'm an intern here."

"An intern! Well, I suggest you try harder to look like a teacher. I couldn't tell you apart from our students."

Sharon replied politely, "I'm sorry if I offended you. But the fact remains that I am an intern and I do belong here."

Deflated, the blunt teacher returned to her place in the line.

Overlook intimidation. Stand tall in the position which you have rightly earned.

"God gave man work, not to burden him, but to bless him, and useful work, willingly, cheerfully, effectively done, has always been the finest expression of the human spirit."
— Walter R. Courtenay

Mirror, Mirror

Tim couldn't remember why he went into teaching thirty years ago. Whatever the reason, it was lost to him now.

He was looking forward to the next few years, only because they would lead out of education and hopefully into something more fulfilling. His apathy was visible—not just to his fellow teachers, but also to the students themselves.

To his colleagues Tim was distant and uninterested. He rarely interacted on any social level. Even cordial greetings were usually met with no more than a groan.

To his students, Tim barked out assignments with all the subtlety of a Marine drill sergeant.

His actions and attitude spoke volumes to his students. Tim communicated through his behavior that teaching was a lousy job and intimidation a powerful motivator. His students came to know classwork as punishment.

What a testimony!

What testimony do you give your students? What work ethic do they see you model in your teaching? What have they learned from watching you?

Self-reflection
clarifies
better than
any mirror.

"One of the best ways to persuade
others is with your ears."
— Dean Rusk

Listening

Have you ever had a conversation with
someone whose responses weren't in response to
your thoughts, but to his own? You know the kind
of person who can't wait for the other person to
stop speaking so he can say what he wants to say?

Steve had the strongest personality on the
textbook selection committee. His opposing points,
which he made frequently, reminded his colleagues
of a lawyer's closing arguments. He was logical,
rational, and a problem solver. However, he
alienated everyone on the committee and usually
intimidated them into reluctant silence.

Steve, as a result, became frustrated with the

committee's lack of enthusiasm. He tried to rally them to a consensus on the issues, but all he perceived was ambivalence.

In actuality, Steve had talked himself right into isolation from the group.

With characteristic passion, he finally said, "We're getting nowhere. What do you want from me?"

Matter-of-factly, one member answered, "A chance to get a word in edgewise."

From this embarrassing experience, Steve learned an important life lesson.

When working on a team effort, think positive and seek resolve in solution oriented terms.

Be honest with yourself and evaluate. Are you being a team player?

"There's only one corner of the universe
you can be certain of improving and
that's your own self."

— Aldous Huxley

Show and Tell

Beth was known for her innovative teaching. She had been chosen "Teacher of the Year" just the year before.

She had become popular and was known for obtaining grants that secure monies to enrich and enhance the educational experience for her students. Sure that others would want to share in her luster, she suggested and offered a workshop for those teachers interested in doing things along a similar vein. She would teach them all she had learned.

Her principal approved, and Beth announced her workshop at the following faculty meeting.

One week later, she stood in her classroom

watching the clock, realizing that no one was coming to her meeting. Just before she packed up for the day, a friend came to see her.

"Are you here for the workshop?" she asked hopefully.

"No. I came to see how it went."

"Well, I guess everyone had other things to do, because no one showed up," Beth said matter-of-factly.

"I'm sorry. Maybe next time you could make it more like a social, and they'll come."

"I wasn't here to be sociable!"

Beth knew as soon as the words left her mouth that her attitude had been all wrong. No wonder no one had shown up for her meeting. She had isolated herself from her colleagues.

Determined to not let that same attitude of pride dictate her behavior again, she nurtured and shared her secrets with her fellow teachers on a personal level and regained their trust and mutual esteem.

If you find yourself frustrated with others because they are failing to meet your expectations, check your own standing first.

"Statistics are no substitute for judgment."
— Henry Clay

Number Crunching

Each year standardized test scores are used to determine whether or not students are succeeding. Districts publish reports ranking their schools according to test performance. Deciphering these statistical reports is difficult at best.

Tim and his family were moving to another city and their realtor had sent him the breakdown of scores on the surrounding area schools.

The reports were complex. He could tell which schools had the highest reading and math scores, but he couldn't tell which schools had the most innovative and caring teachers.

Tim wanted his children to attend a neighborhood school, without having to ride a bus. He wanted them to feel safe, yet part of a bigger community.

With his report in hand, he selected five specific schools and decided to take a trip to visit them. Tim made his final judgments based on the following criteria:

1. Which schools had friendly office staff?

2. Which schools allowed him to freely visit the classrooms?

3. Which schools had principals who were found more often in classrooms than in their offices?

Tim's final choice was a school that ranked good in test score standings but also high in the other things that mattered. Tim's children thrived there and were very happy with the choice their dad had made.

Remember that teaching is more than high test scores; it is also enriching lives.

"The best things and best people
rise out of their separateness;
I'm against a homogenized society
because I want the cream to rise."
— Robert Frost

Dare to Be Different

The quest for equity dilutes the power of
diversity. You can see it all around you. Every child
gets a trophy whether they win or not. Competitions
are only disguised showcases of mediocre talent.
Everything is designed to ensure the satisfaction of
as many as possible.

Standing out for your accomplishments isn't
"in." It might make someone else look bad. In
some places, going above and beyond the call of
duty is actually discouraged.

Are you creating a homogenous classroom? Does the high achiever feel he or she can shine, or is his or her talent shrouded amidst the average?

When we create the same boundaries for everyone, we are ignoring individuality and unique gifts.

Admittedly, in this world of quotas and demographics, it is hard to stand up for diversity.

But think about it. As a teacher, do you believe all teachers should be granted the same rewards? Are you intimidated by the idea of merit pay or teacher-of-the-year awards? Do you scowl at the new teacher with bright ideas? If so, ask yourself why.

Instead of letting your fears paralyze you, let them light a fire of inspiration under you.

Rise to the occasion and dare to be different! Allow some individuality in your students. Only then will you discover their true potential.

"The secret of success is
constancy to purpose."
— Benjamin Disraeli

Stick to Your Goals

It's easy to get distracted from your mission as
a teacher. Your time is limited and the demands
are great.

Good teachers are always on the hunt for new and
better ways to do things. You want to make the lesson
more exciting for your students and for yourself.

Sometimes a change of pace or style can have a
great impact.

Have you ever attended a conference or
workshop that was particularly innovative and
exciting? Did you learn strategies or a new
program that seemed to have S-U-C-C-E-S-S

written all over it?

We all know from experience that just because it's new doesn't mean it is better. And just because it is different doesn't mean it will work.

How can you judge whether or not this new idea is worth trying? Ask yourself these questions:

1. Does this idea inspire me?

2. Will this new technique blend cohesively with my teaching style?

3. Can I incorporate this idea into the classroom and still accomplish my goals with students, or will it become a distraction?

Change simply for the sake of change isn't enough. You need to clearly see a direct connection between the strategy or program and your aspirations for your students.

"Although the world is full of suffering,
it is full also of the overcoming of it."
— Helen Keller

Annie Sullivan

Helen Keller was considered a sort of wild child before Annie Sullivan came to teach and work with her. Her world now dark and silent, Helen thrashed around the house much to her parents' dismay.

After a slow and frustrating start, Helen recognized her first word in sign language—water. It was a triumphant day for both teacher and student.

Soon after, Helen was quick to learn other words. Annie was proud of her student. She could not believe how quickly Helen learned. She called her progress a miracle. Helen's accomplishments were amazing, achieving what seemed to be impossible.

Now that Helen could express her thoughts, the crying fits stopped. She was happy and contented.

Whenever Annie taught her a new word, Helen would throw her arms around her teacher and kiss her.

Teachers of delayed or disabled students can testify to similar miracles. Parents usually bestow undying gratitude to the teacher who unlocks their child's world and gives them hope.

Each child's potential can be unlocked. Each teacher has the key. Are you willing to take the time to find out which key fits?

Your undying commitment may well be met by undying gratitude.

"My business is not to remake myself, but make the absolute best of what God made."
— Robert Browning

Growing

If you've been teaching the same way, under the same conditions for a long time, then burnout could be a possible reality.

And just as you encourage your students to never stop learning, you too must continue to develop, grow, and enrich your life in ways you might have never considered.

If your attitude toward workshops is that they just take you away from your classroom and are not that valuable, then it is time for you to seek out other opportunities for growth.

Commit to attending at least one educational

conference a year, whether you get paid for it or not.

Join an area association and pour over the journals and materials that come with the membership.

If you don't have time to take a university course in current trends and issues, then at least go to the university bookstore and buy a title that looks interesting.

If you feel like you've just been treading water for a few years, decide now to take the plunge. Sometimes you have to immerse yourself into educational and community events in order to feel a part of things again.

A good start is to spend time with teachers who talk about education instead of the ones who complain. Before you know it, you'll remember why you went into teaching in the first place. The love affair can begin again.

Daily make an effort to grow and become your best.

"It is impossible for a man to be made
happy by putting him in a happy place,
unless he be first in a happy state."
— Benjamin Whichcote

Are You Happy?

Jan's previous school was new, full of the latest
technology and innovative teachers. She longed to
go back, but she didn't have enough seniority.

Jan was miserable at Jones Elementary. This
school was old, small, and full of teachers who
were from "the old school." Her frustration grew
until finally she decided to leave.

Moving to a new district was full of promise.
Since her new school was located in the state's
capital, she thought the emphasis on quality would
be evident.

But again, due to lack of seniority, she was placed in a school in a low socio-economic area that was old, rural, and full of teachers stuck in their old routines.

"I want to go back to my old district," she cried to her husband. "They were more professional there."

Jan continued to move from school to school, never satisfied. The fact was that even in her first school, she wasn't happy either.

The bottom line is that Jan just wasn't a happy person, and geographical relocations and new circumstances were never going to change that issue. Jan had never had the self-discovery that true personal happiness comes from within.

Take a look at your world. Are you content? If not, take a look inside. Are you happy with who you see?

Attitude is everything! If you are unhappy with where God has placed you, look inside your heart.

"If a friend is in trouble,
don't annoy him by asking him if
there's anything you can do. Think of
something appropriate, and do it."
— E.W. Howe

Friends

Cindy and Sharon were expecting a baby at the same time this school year. Because they were friends, it made it all the more special.

Then one day Sharon didn't come to work. She had miscarried over the weekend. Cindy's sadness for her friend turned into apprehension as she wondered what to say once she returned. She knew she'd be a constant reminder to Sharon of her loss.

When Sharon did return, she walked like a ghost through the school's hallways. No one spoke to her, let alone acknowledged her loss. They didn't know what to say, so they said nothing. Even Cindy found herself avoiding her friend. She knew Sharon was hurting; she just didn't know what to do about it.

Two weeks later, Cindy happened upon Sharon in the teacher's lounge during her free period. Sharon was supposed to be in class, yet she was here, crying. Cindy instinctively comforted her friend, but then realized Sharon's class was unsupervised.

Sharon was paralyzed with grief and couldn't function. Assuring Sharon that everything would be all right, Cindy ran to the classroom just after the late bell.

Cindy took care of Sharon's class that period. It was all she could think to do, yet it was just what Sharon needed from her.

Use compassion when dealing with fellow teachers, and act swiftly when duty calls.

Never use words when action is required.

"There are only two lasting bequests
we can hope to give our children.
One of these is roots; the other, wings."
— Hodding Carter

Louisa May Alcott

Louisa May Alcott was a teacher's kid.

Her lively temperament suited her father's unorthodox teaching methods during the 1830s.

Bronson Alcott had started several schools during Louisa's childhood. Louisa spent much time in her father's schools, even before she was of school age herself. Some of her fondest memories were of playing in her father's schools.

Bronson Alcott believed in making lessons as exciting and interesting as possible. Alcott's schools always started out quite promising, but because people did not understand his new methods of education, many grew uncomfortable and withdrew their children from the schools.

But for Louisa and the students who were allowed to remain, their futures were transformed. Bronson Alcott brought the elements of adventure, curiosity, persistence, and creativity to his students as part of the learning process.

Louisa learned how to give of herself before others as she watched her father sacrifice for teaching.

His love for teaching touched her deep inside. His support for her writing gave her fledgling career wings.

As teachers, never bridle your enthusiasm for teaching in front of your students. Let them see you boldly go forth to shape minds and mold futures.

Transform futures with adventure and creativity!

"Imagination is more important
than knowledge."
— Albert Einstein

The Right Answer

"What would it be like if . . ." Miss Chandler
asked her wide-eyed sixth graders, ". . . if we
suddenly had to live without electricity?"

Silence. No hands rising. Questioning looks.

"Come on," she coaxed. "Just yell out ideas."
Again, silence.

"Okay, I'll start you off." Miss Chandler
proceeded to list three things they would have to
do if they didn't have electricity anymore. Slowly
but surely, the students sat up a little taller, and the
answers started coming.

Afraid that they didn't have the right answer,

her students were reluctant to participate in the creative process.

Schools have trained students that the right answer is the one that matters most. So what you see on students' faces when you ask thought-provoking questions is usually fear!

How can you make your classroom a safe place to dream?

It's more than creative bulletin boards and playing classical music in the background. It's your attitude.

If you believe that there is value in the process, then you must communicate that to your students. They have to know they can give a wrong answer in order to find the right one. And they need to know that sometimes there is more than one right answer.

Most importantly, they need to know that there will be times in life when no answers are available, but seeking for them is always okay.

Is your classroom a safe place to dream?

"A good laugh is sunshine in a house."
— Thackeray

Laugh

Justin was the class clown. There wasn't a day that went by that he didn't interrupt some lesson with his quick wit. He saw "funny" written all over everything.

You have to be careful with the class clown. He or she can easily take over your class and Mr. Watkins had decided early on that this would never happen in his class.

But it became a challenge to Justin to make Mr. Watkins laugh. Justin realized that it had to be carefully planned. He also realized that it could happen more easily if he completed all his work so Mr. Watkins wouldn't have anything to complain about.

What Justin didn't know is that Mr. Watkins was struggling every day not to laugh. He didn't want to give Justin the satisfaction.

But Justin was hillarious! The more Mr. Watkins avoided eye contact, the more Justin attracted attention to himself. It was becoming a stressful situation for Mr. Watkins. He began getting tension headaches and would end the day in a grumpy mood.

Then one day it happened. Mr. Watkins let go and laughed out loud!

The class was shocked; the clown was jubilant!

The teacher was relieved.

Headaches gone, Mr. Watkins realized that laughter really was the best medicine. He decided to take a dose each day.

If handled well, laughter can be used to your advantage.

Let them see you laugh, and you let them see your heart.

"Every child is an artist.
The problem is how to remain
an artist once he grows up."
— Pablo Picasso

Dr. Seuss

Ted Geisel's talent for writing and drawing
didn't always impress his teachers. Once in art
class, the future Dr. Seuss turned his painting
upside down to look at it. He wasn't exactly sure
why he did it, but he found out later this is how an
artist can check a painting's balance. If the painting
is balanced, it will look good upside down or right
side up. His art teacher, however, thought Ted was
fooling around and claimed that real artists never
turned their paintings upside down.

"That teacher wanted me to draw the world as
it is," Ted said, "and I wanted to draw things as I

saw them."

Ted rejected his art teacher's advice not to pursue art as a career. He resolved right then and there to be an artist someday.

Even though he was shy, uncoordinated, and had a unique sense of humor, his stubbornness is what pushed him into the spotlight.

What does an artist look like? He may not be the pretty one, the graceful one, or the evident genius.

He may be the one you least expect to succeed because he follows the beat of a different drummer. Listen for that offbeat, and pay closer attention to the drummer.

Encourage the artistic soul discovered in your students.

"A place for everything, and
everything in its place."
— Samuel Smiles

Order! Order!

Teaching is one of the few professions that if
you're absent, an immediate replacement must be
found for you.

It takes more than written substitute plans for
a stranger to effectively teach your class in your
absence. It also takes organization.

Do you know a teacher whose room is one big
pile? Whose desk isn't evident to the human eye?
Whose supplies spill into crevices and corners and
whose files are in name only?

That teacher puts a substitute in peril when he
or she takes over a class.

How can a teacher help a substitute? Leave directions. Let the substitute know where the teacher's manuals are. Where the grade book is. Where the supplies lay hidden.

When substitutes have to rely on students in order to find things, then they appear helpless. They aren't able to adequately cover the material and take control of the classroom. They feel frustrated and may never come back.

Teachers complain that they are not considered professionals by the world.

How professional is your classroom by the world's standards? Your room is a direct reflection on you.

Need help getting organized? Find someone whose classroom you admire and ask for help.

"Treat people as if they were what they ought to be and you help them to become what they are capable of being."
—Johann Wolfgang von Goethe

Reach for the Stars

Barb was used to having children with special needs in her fourth grade classroom. She knew how to modify the curriculum to fit her students individually.

Parents were appreciative of her open-mindedness, and their children succeeded in her class.

One year, Barb was faced with a child whose needs she had never encountered before.

Chris had one of the highest IQ's she had ever seen. He scored four years above his grade level on standardized tests. But Chris had become lazy, and would only do the bare minimum. Even so, his bare minimum was still higher than the rest of his class. He got straight A's, but Barb knew he could do more.

Barb decided to raise the bar on Chris. She defined for him a separate list of expectations. At first Chris balked at the change. His comfort level was threatened. For the first time in his short academic career, Chris wasn't sure he'd get an *A*. He had to work for it.

After a few weeks of careful monitoring, Chris had regained his passion for learning. He began to crave challenge, and Barb gave it to him. She kept him on his toes, and he kept her on hers.

Never let your students accept the status quo. Push them; let them taste the satisfaction and exhilaration that come from a hunger for knowledge.

Teach your students to reach, and they'll never stay on the ground.

157

"The good life, as I conceive it,
is a happy life. I do not mean that if
you are good you will be happy—I mean
that if you are happy you will be good."
— Bertrand Russell

Babe Ruth

A few months after his seventh birthday, George (Babe) Ruth was labeled a juvenile delinquent and was sent to the St. Mary's Industrial School for Boys. The years he spent at St. Mary's turned his life around.

At St. Mary's, George had to follow a strict regimen of activities that included religious instruction, academic studies, industrial training, and athletics. George, of course, excelled on the athletic field.

But it was more than athletics that saved George Ruth.

Brother Matthias took the boy under his wing and encouraged him to take advantage of his talents. Matthias was a fair man. George, who was considered one of the school's biggest trouble-makers, respected him. Matthias, who was responsible for putting Ruth on the right track, gave George the love and attention he never got from his own father.

Ruth later said that Brother Matthias was "the greatest man I've ever known."

Is there a Babe Ruth in your classroom? A troublemaker whose talent has yet to be harnessed? You know who he is. He's the one you wish would be absent, but never is.

Maybe you will be the teacher to point him or her in the right direction.

Give your students a chance, and they might well make you proud.

"Nothing has a better effect
upon children than praise."
— Sir P. Sidney

Positive Reinforcement

George felt like he was in a no-win situation.
They cut his position, and the only way he could
stay at his school was to take a new position as a
dropout prevention teacher. He really didn't want
to, but he felt like he had no choice.

He was miserable, and it showed. Other
teachers commented that George's classroom was
like a morgue—cold, sterile, and much too quiet.
George got through the curriculum and kept order.
But the day could never end soon enough for him
or his students.

Then one day George received a letter from a
parent. He cringed upon opening it but found

instead a treasure. This parent was incredibly grateful that her son was finally learning and that there was a teacher her son could count on.

The letter completely changed George's outlook. He felt appreciated.

For the first time that year, he smiled upon entering his classroom. Not surprisingly, his students smiled back!

As a teacher, you appreciate affirmation from others, because it sends the message that you are reaching your students and doing your job well.

You know how well you do when you're complimented; don't forget to share the wealth with your students.

"The rain falls on all the fields,
but crops grow only in those
that have been tilled and sown."
— Chinese Proverb

Success

Teacher in-service is a necessary evil.

With so many changes being implemented, it's difficult to stay up on what is expected. Training is demanded and budgets are crunched in order to meet the needs.

Workshops take up almost every free moment. When you sit in an auditorium full of hundreds of teachers (who would rather be somewhere else) and learn about a promising new strategy, have you ever noticed that only a few actually carry out the recommendations?

It depends on whether or not a teacher is returning to a school that values innovation and embraces change. It depends on whether there is an administrator who frees up teacher time so they can employ new approaches. It depends on the needs of the teacher.

How similar is this phenomenon to what happens in your classroom every day? You teach a new concept and only a small percentage latch onto it right away.

The future success of your students will depend on whether or not you have created an environment that welcomes questions. It depends on whether you give them the time they need to master topics. It depends on whether you're meeting the needs of your students.

Set your students up for success, not failure.

"People should be free to find or
make for themselves the kinds of
educational experiences they want
their children to have."
— John Holt

Teddy Roosevelt

None of the Roosevelt children went to public
school. When they were little, their aunt taught
them their lessons. As they got older, tutors were
hired to educate the children.

Mittie Roosevelt was devoted to her children,
and also instilled a strong spirit of adventure and
daring in them—especially young Teddy.

This was particularly important since Teddy
suffered from more than his share of illnesses.

His asthma made it impossible for him to take

part in the lively games the rest of the family enjoyed. He spent much of his time alone. But Teddy was bright and inquisitive, so his mother encouraged him to spend his time reading and writing. His mother's devotion as his teacher gave Teddy a well-rounded education.

His love for nature was fed by books and first-hand meetings of real-life explorers. His thirst for adventure was fueled by his mother's provision and made him the rough-riding president history recorded.

Do you know a child whose parents have decided to school him at home? Instead of being defensive about their choice, do what you can to make it the best choice possible. Offer your expertise and ideas. Be a help.

You know the commitment it takes to be a teacher. Respect the parents who make that commitment themselves.

"Until you try, you don't know
what you can't do."
— Henry James

In the Spotlight

Candice was a teacher who wanted to be an integral part of her new school. She had experience in yearbook, chorus, and writing. So working with these clubs would be natural for her.

Weeks after the school year began, a teacher left unexpectedly. Not only did she leave a hole in the language department, but now they needed a new drama club sponsor.

The principal approached Candice with the job, since she knew Candice was looking to get involved. But Candice had no experience with drama. She was reluctant to take on such a big job.

Her principal encouraged her to try. She could always quit if she wanted to, so Candice tried.

What she found out was that she loved drama! She was good at directing. Her organizational skills and attention to detail made that year's production one of the most professional the school had ever done.

When the students presented her with a dozen roses at the end of opening night, Candice couldn't believe she was standing on stage being applauded for efforts she never knew she could bring forth.

When you find yourself in the spotlight, even if you were pushed there, you may find you like it and actually deserve to be there.

Some of the best discoveries are made when we simply try.

"Try to say the very thing you really mean,
the whole of it, nothing more or less
or other than what you really mean.
That is the whole art and joy of words."
— C.S. Lewis

Words

Deborah was easily intimidated by parents, especially those who were the most vocal. Fearing the way a principal might view her, she avoided a documented parent complaint in her records at all costs. Deborah followed the path of least resistance and ignored minor student disturbances.

Her conferences were always a mere formality. If a problem was avoidable, she'd avoid it. A certain situation, however, changed her perspective.

A colleague's child was in Deborah's advanced

math class. Never expecting this to be a problem, Deborah was quite surprised that the student was not performing to the class standard. In fact, he was failing. Upon checking his records, she found that he actually belonged in another class.

She met with the mother and fellow teacher about the situation, only to discover that she had manipulated the situation and purposefully placed him in that class.

After going 'round and 'round for an hour about what help the student needed, Deborah decided to cut to the chase. "What I mean to say is that Steven really belongs in an average class."

As expected, her comment didn't go over well, but the information was received. They came to terms and moved him to the correct class, and as Deborah expected he excelled.

Following professional ethics sometimes takes courage. What's the alternative?

Never compromise the truth for fear.

"Work is love made visible."
— Kahlil Gibran

Love Your Job

Ellen knew she wanted to be a teacher since the first grade. She could remember setting her bedroom up like a classroom and making her four siblings be the students.

Her first grade teacher, Mrs. Robinson, loved her students. They in turn loved her and loved to learn. Ellen wanted to instill that same love in others, so she became a teacher.

All agree that teachers don't get paid enough. You have to be in it for more than money. You have to love to teach.

Ellen always felt on fire when she was teaching.

When a lesson clicked, it was an exhilarating feeling.

Once in a while she'd give students a chance to teach the class. They knew the material well enough to make a presentation. Those who volunteered did so out of desire, not out of outside pressure. She could see future teachers among her students. She could see their love for learning.

So when the union couldn't negotiate a higher raise or the budget was cut again and her materials were meager, she was still happy.

Ellen was doing what she loved, and she did it well.

Remember to teach from your heart, not from duty.

When you do what you love, you do it well, no matter the circumstances.

"There is no greater delight than to be conscious of sincerity on self-examination."
— Mencius

Support

Laura was new to teaching. Vicki was a veteran teacher and had been at Lake Elementary for many years.

Vicki took it upon herself to show Laura "the ropes" of their school. She pointed out its strengths as well as its weaknesses. She provided inside information on the school's culture, took Laura under her wing, and they quickly became good friends.

New ways of doing things defined Vicki's teaching style. She was a creative fund-raiser, a strong student advocate, and an excellent communicator with parents.

Laura was learning much from Vicki and was especially appreciative. But she was uncomfortable with Vicki's critical nature of others.

It quickly became evident to Laura that the other staff members were noticeably uneasy with Vicki's critical nature, as well. Laura knew she needed to talk to Vicki about her aggressive quest for excellence, yet felt awkward approaching the subject being the "new kid on the block."

Timidly and reluctantly, Laura spoke with Vicki.

Vicki's silence made it difficult to tell how she was handling the insight. But after a few days of soul-searching, Vicki returned to Laura and said, "Thank you for your honesty. I was looking at the other teachers as 'them' instead of 'us.' "

In teaching it is important to remember that your colleagues can be a great support system. Support them in all things.

Be a supporter of the team, not an opponent.

"People only see what they
are prepared to see."
— Ralph Waldo Emerson

Do It Your Way

Teaching eighth grade science was Susan's passion. She effectively covered the content and inspired her students to ask questions. Most days she could be found at the center of huddled eighth graders who were trying to catch a glimpse of some scientific phenomenon.

Her supervisor, Mr. Dawson, was from "the old school." He saw disorder when students crowded around her. He saw unprofessional conduct in her enthusiasm. He didn't see what he expected to see: students working quietly, and a teacher lecturing from the overhead projector.

During a conference, the assistant principal warned Susan of his forthcoming evaluation. She muzzled her disbelief as she strained to maintain the appearance of professionalism.

Realizing that it was his perception that her students weren't learning, she knew she had to prove otherwise. Calmly, she explained her philosophy and invited him to return the next day to her class.

That next day, she carefully orchestrated a lesson that showcased her students' grasp of a scientific method. They performed beautifully as if on cue. Once Mr. Dawson was satisfied, Susan was free to teach her own way.

Fair or not, there will be times in teaching that you too will have to satisfy the doubts of others and prove yourself.

Sometimes you need to give others what they want before you can do what you want.

"Take the attitude of a student. Never
be too big to ask questions. Never
know too much to learn something new."
— Og Mandino

Involuntary Transfer

Jan's involuntary transfer to an elementary
school was difficult. Not only did she prefer middle
school, but she felt inadequate to teach at that
level. Just because she was certified in elementary
didn't mean she wanted to teach it.

Teaching in a self-contained classroom all day
was quite an adjustment for Jan. Her first method
of coping was to keep to herself and observe.

After the first grading period, she realized there
was more to being an elementary teacher than
wearing theme jewelry and giving out stickers. Her

demands on her students were too high and she knew it. She could tell from their faces when she assigned research reports. She could tell from their parents as note after note came in with complaints. She just didn't know what to do about it all.

During her third grade team meeting, Jan sat and listened to Kathy, a first year teacher. Kathy's students loved her. Her room was bursting with energy and creativity. Even her discipline problems were minimal.

How does she do that? Jan wondered. Then in a moment of utter humility she said it aloud, "How do you do that?"

That was the beginning of a beautiful friendship and a successful school year!

Don't be afraid to ask questions of team members you admire or to share tips with someone new.

> Find someone who is doing what you want to be doing well, and ask them how they do it.

"The important thing is
not to stop questioning."
— Albert Einstein

Why?

You encourage your students to ask questions. You tell them that the only stupid question is the one that's not asked. You try to create a non-threatening classroom environment in which students feel safe to ask questions.

There is a question, however, that you cringe at when you hear it: "Why?" A question that disputes the choices you've made about what to teach can put you on the defense.

Contrary to popular belief, questioning the status quo is not always disrespectful. There are times when it causes a teacher to stop and think—to question oneself.

How often do you evaluate how you're doing in the classroom?

Forget the annual evaluation your principal conducts. Ask yourself what you're doing and why you're doing it.

In turn, question the status quo at your school. Look for relevance in every decision. Look for pertinence in every choice. If you are on a committee, don't be afraid to ask, "Why this fund-raiser? Why this time? Why this way? Why this reward? Why this trip?"

Ask the questions everyone thinks about but never has the courage to speak. Ask the hard questions.

Ask, "Why?"

Define your goals; then every once in a while ask yourself, *Am I on track?*

"Act enthusiastic and you
become enthusiastic."
— Dale Carnegie

Power of Positive Thinking

Cecile made a deal with her seventh grade class on the first day of school. She said, "I'll warn you when I'm having a bad day, so you warn me when you're having a bad day. That way, we'll both give each other a little extra grace."

This system of mutual respect actually worked in the beginning. If Cecile had a particularly bad morning, she would announce, "I got very little sleep last night and I'm grouchy."

By the same token, a student would say, "I had a fight with my mom this morning; I'm not in a good mood." Each side would then give the other a wider berth.

Unfortunately, this plan began to backfire. She noticed that more and more kids were complaining. They were all concentrating on the negatives in their lives. Even students who were usually upbeat began to complain about their day. It had all gone too far.

Cecile decided a new approach was in order.

She pushed "smile and the world smiles with you" instead. It took a lot of patience, but slowly the class took on a more positive attitude and their performance improved.

What positive imprint can you leave on your class today?

Reinforce a positive attitude within your students.

"Shoot for the moon. Even if you miss it you will land among the stars."
— Les (Lester Louis) Brown

Expectations

The challenge of motivating students occupies much of a teacher's time and resources. Constant thoughts of, *If I could just get into their hearts, I know I could get through to them.*

You hope they care enough to try and excel. You certainly want them to excel!

It took until graduate school for Anna to realize the power of expectations.

Her professor told them that he expected to see only A's and B's out of his students. He spelled out what to do to get a *B* and what to do to get an *A*. Assuming they all wanted A's, he went into the greatest detail, outlining specifically how to get one.

Could this work in my classroom? Anna wondered.

To her amazement the first time she tried this, a quarter of her students expressed the desire to work toward an *A*. Three-quarters chose to work for a *B*.

By the end of the year, more than 80 percent of her students actually achieved higher grades than they did the period before!

This exercise in expectations was triumphant—for both the students and the teacher.

Keep your expectations for your students high. Mix those expectations with large doses of encouragement and you will discover a class full of achievers!

Never underestimate the power of expectation.

"There is a great man, who makes very many feel small. But the real great man is the man who makes every man feel great."
— G.K. Chesterton

The Note

Joyce could never do anything to please Mrs. Raymond. After three years at Charter Middle School, she walked the halls in timid avoidance of her principal. Three humiliating observations and conferences made Joyce feel insignificant and insecure.

The next year another principal was transferred to their school, and like before, Joyce avoided contact with her.

Then one morning, Mrs. Baker, the new principal, popped her head into Joyce's room. She took a seat at the back of the class unnoticed by the students, and stayed for the entire lesson!

Joyce worried. This observation was unannounced. She was sick at the thought of what was to come.

Later that day, Joyce found a note in her mailbox.

"Thanks for a delightful morning. It always encourages me to see a good teacher in action. Keep up the good work!"

This small act of kindness encouraged Joyce and several other teachers like her, to stay on at the school and continue to perform their best.

A change in principals almost always generates some staff turnover in a school. Those who fell in line with the previous administration are apprehensive about the changes that are sure to come. Yet most times, change is good.

Try to keep an open mind regarding change. Don't let your fears hinder bright possibilities.

Remember how you benefit from simple acts of kindness and bestow those same gifts on your students.

"Behind every able man there
are always other able men."
— Chinese Proverb

Alone

Susan sat alone in her classroom eating her
lunch as she did every day. The only sound was the
clicking of the ceiling fan which was the only
means of relief on this sticky May day.

Her students loved their innovative and creative
teacher. She could turn mundane facts into lessons
of real life intrigue. She could motivate unwilling
children in a single year. And when she was
nominated "teacher of the year," no one was
surprised. But just like Superman, this super teacher
felt very much alone amongst her colleagues.

Susan was not the only exceptional teacher at her
school. She was just the one who gained the most

attention. Attention from the local media. Attention from supervisors and from students' parents.

Then why does she dine alone each day? Peer jealousy. It infects even the best of schools. It can destroy healthy relationships and kill morale.

How do you reverse its effects? One way is by reaching outside of yourself to others. Another way is to esteem others above yourself.

You can't create a shared vision by being a lone ranger. Remember to include others in your plans, and they will remember to include you.

If building yourself up is tearing others down, then it's time to rethink your priorities.

"If you don't say anything,
you won't be called upon to repeat it."
— Calvin Coolidge

The Tyrant

Judy had been looking forward to this school year with great anticipation. Prior to that first day, she tried to speak with her new principal. As school social worker, she needed to know what Mrs. Ricker expected from her.

After three unreturned phone calls and two unsuccessful visits, Judy decided she would wait until she saw Mrs. Ricker that first day.

Just before lunch Judy was called into the principal's office. "Miss Wilson, we have a problem."

Before Judy could even respond, Mrs. Ricker continued, "I expected you to contact me personally before ever setting foot on my campus!"

Judy sat there in confused silence. "How could the district send us such an inexperienced social worker?"

The only thing Judy could do now was to pray that her composure would remain intact. She turned to leave, but Mrs. Ricker's words pursued her. "And if I were you, I'd stay out of my way."

Not all educators will be as happy to be in education as you are. And there will be times when you will not see eye to eye, but stay focused on your true mission.

The only way to have peace in the midst of adversity is to silently forgive any trespasses and move on.

When entering a new school, get to know your leadership and operate within those parameters.

"The smile of God is victory."
— John Greenleaf Whittier

Approval Rating

Teresa didn't fully comprehend the scope of her accountability as a beginning teacher. Not only did she seek the approval of her principal, but students, parents, the community at large, and the state all had a say in how well she was doing her job—how well she was teaching.

Trying to please everyone became exhausting and frustrating. If she pleased her students, sometimes the principal wasn't happy. If she pleased the parents, sometimes the kids were disappointed.

There were days when it felt like a no-win situation. She soon learned in her attempts to please everyone, that it was not only impossible, it was paralyzing.

You may choose the road of inaction instead of innovation, just to be on the safe side. Inside you will know you could do more or do better, but you let the approval rating from others tie your hands.

Discovering and doing what is best needs to be your quest. After all, what matters most is that you are serving your students' needs.

Never compromise your principles. Stand firm, and truth will be served.

Do your best and take pride in your decisions.

"People need to see how much
agreement is possible between
seemingly intractable opponents."
—Robert Redford

Satisfaction Guaranteed?

Janice sighed heavily as she hung up the
phone. Mrs. Baxter, the mother of a student with
special needs, wanted a conference—again.

It seemed that she couldn't please this mother.
Although their meetings always ended on a
positive note, Janice was beginning to wonder what
she could do to avoid them altogether.

This year had definitely been one with unusual
challenges in Janice's classroom, and to be truthful,
Mrs. Baxter usually had valid concerns.

This conference began just as all the rest—Mrs.
Baxter restating her son's needs; Janice restating her

desire to meet his needs. But this time, Mrs. Baxter had a new question ready. "What level of satisfaction should a parent expect from your class?"

What a loaded question! Janice was speechless. Mrs. Baxter continued, "We both know that 100 percent is not realistic. Nothing and no one is perfect."

Mrs. Baxter went on to explain that after some soul searching she knew that her own unusually high expectations had created some of the frustrations she was feeling over her son's school year.

Mrs. Baxter's humility struck a chord with Janice. She turned the question around. What were her expectations of parents? Were they realistic? Janice knew she had some of her own soul searching to do.

A willingness to put forth the effort to understand each other opened the door for a wonderful relationship between Janice and Mrs. Baxter.

> Make understanding your priority before trying to be understood.

"There's few things as uncommon
as common sense."
—Frank McKinney Hubbard

Mother's Advice

by Ailene Doherty

Ailene's mother had a happy outlook on life that glistened in her hazel eyes and shined through her welcoming smile. In her lilting Scotch-Irish accent, she often offered practical advice.

As a new teacher, Ailene was beginning to appreciate this advice more than ever before. One weekend, Ailene told her mother that her principal was punishing the students too severely. After she had expressed in vibrant tones what she would say to that harsh man, her mother gently corrected, "Little said is easily mended, my dear."

The most amusing bit of advice her mother

had given was "Don't make two bites of a cherry." That is, don't make something more difficult than it actually is. Ailene would think of this adage when she caught herself entering one grade at a time into her grade book rather than waiting until she had corrected the whole set; or when she found herself standing at the copy machine for the fourth time in one day rather than planning to make all her copies at once.

Undoubtedly, valuable lessons in life can be learned through the wisdom and experience of others. Treasure the advice of those who are close to you; they could prove to be your most valuable resources.

Allow your opinions to be enriched by the insight of others.

"I cannot give you the formula for success,
but I can give you the formula for failure—
try to please everybody."
— Herbert Bayard Swope

Easy to Please

With only three years left until he retired, Mr. Latham longed for a peaceful, problem-free year. He was in a school he had led for eight years. This was his last stop. He wanted to leave it on a successful note.

Since his elementary school had more than 800 students, the district built a new school to house the ever-increasing South District student population.

This welcome relief turned into a nightmare as angry parents petitioned re-zoning committees. Latham was flooded with special attendance permits daily, but this was just the beginning of his frustrations.

Long awaited construction at his school had finally begun. However, it displaced many classes and lasted much longer than ever projected.

Teachers were frustrated and parents were even more frustrated. The kids seemed fine. The adults were having all the problems.

Long meetings and lengthy correspondence occupied much of his time. His attempts to please the multitudes were met with skepticism and distrust. At the end of the year, Latham knew it hadn't been his best. Mr. Latham began to wonder if this should be his last year. He thought again and decided that next year would be better. He decided to lead the situations instead of letting the situations lead him.

Upon what gauge are you basing your goals and decisions?

Follow your goals, not the path which follows frustration.

"Kindness is a language which the deaf
can hear and the blind can see."
— Mark Twain

Smile!

by Ailene Doherty

She was about twenty years old, discouraged, and lonely. Maybe she had just been turned down at a job interview, or maybe the young man she was in love with had just told her that everything between them was over. Life was not worth living to her.

The newspaper only stated that a young woman jumped off the Brooklyn Bridge. The note in her jacket read, "If anyone smiles at me today, I won't kill myself."

But nobody did.

She jumped into the swirling waters below.

An immediate reaction upon reading this account is to criticize the people who saw her, but ignored her.

Think instead, *How often do I become so engrossed in my students' passing the Regents exam that I forget to smile?*

Remembering what a smile might have done for that young lady on the Brooklyn Bridge makes us as teachers realize something.

Although your smile may not save a life, it could change a teenager's attitude toward life—even if for only one day.

Your smile could be just what your students need today.

"Facts as facts do not always create a spirit
of reality, because reality is a spirit."
— G.K. Chesterton

George Washington

George Washington's formal education began at the age of seven. Seven was the usual age for teaching children to read and write and to handle numbers. Virginia, like most of the colonies, had no public schools. Most children studied at home.

George's education was a practical one. He learned arithmetic to help him keep accounts and geometry to prepare him for surveying.

He liked to read books that would teach him something useful or give him pleasure. However, his formal education stopped in his early teens. Whatever he learned after that, came from worldly experience, conversation, or reading.

George Washington was one of the few presidents whose formal schooling did not go beyond the level of elementary school. But he never stopped learning from life.

Although you may not be in a position to teach only relevant subjects, try to teach what you have in a relative manner. Answer the question, "So what?" before it is asked. Children remember things that are tied to real life.

Give your students lessons that you've related to current issues. These are the lessons they'll remember the rest of their lives.

Instead of teaching for the next millennium, teach for today.

To furnish the
means of
acquiring knowledge
is ... the greatest
benefit that can
be conferred
upon mankind.

— John Quincy Adams